XML

D0191282

Andrew H. Watt

in **10** Minutes

800 East 96th St., Indianapolis, Indiana, 46240 USA

Sams Teach Yourself XML in 10 Minutes

Copyright © 2003 by Sams Publishing

International Standard Book Number: 0-672-32471-7

Library of Congress Catalog Card Number: 2002110227

Printed in the United States of America

First Printing: October 2002

13 12 11 10 09   14 13 12 11 10 9 8

Trademarks

All terms mentioned in this book that are known to be trademarks or service marks have been appropriately capitalized. Sams Publishing cannot attest to the accuracy of this information. Use of a term in this book should not be regarded as affecting the validity of any trademark or service mark.

Warning and Disclaimer

Every effort has been made to make this book as complete and as accurate as possible, but no warranty or fitness is implied. The information provided is on an "as is" basis. The author and the publisher shall have neither liability nor responsibility to any person or entity with respect to any loss or damages arising from the information contained in this book.

Bulk Sales

Sams Publishing offers excellent discounts on this book when ordered in quantity for bulk purchases or special sales. For more information, please contact

U.S. Corporate and Government Sales
1-800-382-3419
corpsales@pearsontechgroup.com

For sales outside of the U.S., please contact

International Sales
international@pearsoned.com

EXECUTIVE EDITOR
Michael Stephens

ACQUISITIONS EDITOR
Todd Green

DEVELOPMENT EDITOR
Kevin Howard

MANAGING EDITOR
Charlotte Clapp

PROJECT EDITOR
George E. Nedeff

COPY EDITOR
Krista Hansing

INDEXER
Sandra Henselmeier

TECHNICAL EDITORS
Steve Heckler
Mary C. Ecsedy

TEAM COORDINATOR
Lynne Williams

MULTIMEDIA DEVELOPER
Dan Scherf

INTERIOR DESIGNER
Gary Adair

COVER DESIGNER
Aren Howell

Table of Contents

PART 2   Manipulating XML

PART 3   Programming XML

PART 4   Where XML Is Going

About the Author

Andrew Watt is an independent consultant and author with knowledge and interest in XML and graphics topics. He is the author of *Designing SVG Web Graphics* (New Riders, 2001) and *XPath Essentials* (John Wiley & Sons, 2002). He is a co-author of *XML Schema Essentials* (John Wiley & Sons, 2002), *Sams Teach Yourself JavaScript in 21 Days* (Sams, 2002), and *SVG Unleashed* (Sams, 2002). He is also a contributing author to *Platinum Edition Using XHTML, XML, and Java 2* (Que, 2000), *Professional XML, Second Edition* (Wrox Press, 2001), *Professional XSL* (Wrox Press, 2001), *Professional XML Meta Data* (Wrox Press, 2001), and *Special Edition Using XML, Second Edition* (Que, 2002).

Dedication

I would like to dedicate this book to the memory of my late father, George Alec Watt, a very special human being.

Acknowledgments

I would like to thank all the people at Sams Publishing who have made this book possible. Any book is the work of a team, not simply of a single person.

I would like to thank Todd Green and George Nedeff for keeping progress from idea to completion on course. I am grateful to Kevin Howard for careful developing, and Krista Hansing for concise editing.

I am also grateful to Steve Heckler for all his sensible suggestions. I couldn't take them all on board in a book of this size, but they were appreciated.

We Want to Hear from You!

As the reader of this book, *you* are our most important critic and commentator. We value your opinion and want to know what we're doing right, what we could do better, what areas you'd like to see us publish in, and any other words of wisdom you're willing to pass our way.

As an executive editor for Sams Publishing, I welcome your comments. You can email or write me directly to let me know what you did or didn't like about this book—as well as what we can do to make our books better.

Please note that I cannot help you with technical problems related to the *topic* of this book. We do have a User Services group, however, where I will forward specific technical questions related to the book.

When you write, please be sure to include this book's title and author as well as your name, email address, and phone number. I will carefully review your comments and share them with the author and editors who worked on the book.

Email: feedback@samspublishing.com

Mail: Michael Stephens
            Sams Publishing
            201 West 103rd Street
            Indianapolis, IN 46290 USA

For more information about this book or another Sams Publishing title, visit our Web site at www.samspublishing.com. Type the ISBN (excluding hyphens) or the title of a book in the Search field to find the page you're looking for.

Introduction

XML, the Extensible Markup Language, is the basis of many key technologies on the Web and many growing areas of software development. An understanding of at least the basics of XML is essential for an increasing number of Web developers and software developers.

XML bears many similarities to HTML, but it is sufficiently different to cause problems for many newcomers to XML. To write XML code that won't cause an XML parser to choke, you need to get many things right. Some are simple—for example, XML is case sensitive. Others are more subtle. It's important that you get on top of these issues right at the beginning of using XML.

This book teaches you how an XML document is correctly formed— "well-formed," in XML jargon—and how to make use of several of the key XML-related technologies, including XPath, XSLT, the Document Object Model, SAX, and the W3C XML Schema. By the time you finish reading this book, you will understand what these XML-related technologies do and will have grasped many key facts about each of these important technologies so that you can begin to use them for yourself.

Who Is *Sams Teach Yourself XML in 10 Minutes* For?

This book is for you if

- You are new to XML and you want to get a handle on what XML is really about.

- You want to quickly learn the key facts about using XML and its important associated technologies.

- You want to know how to create well-formed XML.

- You want to get a handle on Document Type Definitions (DTDs).

- You want to understand how you can create HTML from XML using XSLT.

- You want to be able to change the structure of an XML document using XSLT.

- You want to learn the basics of programming XML using the Document Object Model and the Simple API for XML (SAX).

- You want to understand the basics of how W3C XML Schema works.

What This Book Covers

This book shows you how an XML document is correctly structured. It also explains and demonstrates how to write XML so that it is well-formed and, therefore, acceptable to an XML parser.

XML is full of jargon, so new terms are explained as they are introduced. The book also has a glossary that explains or reminds you of what many terms mean and when they are used.

You'll be introduced to Document Type Definitions (DTD), which are used to define the allowed structure of a class of XML documents. You'll also learn about using entities in XML, to allow reuse of XML content.

In addition, the book discusses and demonstrates the use of Cascading Style Sheets (CSS) and Extensible Stylesheet Language Transformations (XSLT). You'll also be introduced to linking in XML using the XML Linking Language (XLink) and the XML Pointer Language (XPointer).

The book goes on to cover Scalable Vector Graphics (SVG), and it demonstrates programming XML using the Document Object Model and the Simple API for XML. The final chapter of the book introduces W3C XML Schema, a schema technology that goes beyond the capabilities of the DTD.

Of course, a book of this length can't tell you everything about XML and its associated family of technologies. You're pointed to sources of further information on XML in Appendix A, "XML Online Resources."

What You Need to Use This Book

You don't need expensive tools to create XML code similar to the code you see in this book. If you want, you can use a plain text editor such as Windows Notepad. However, an XML-aware editor such as XML Writer (a 30-day free trial download is available at www.xmlwriter.net) is better.

You will need XSLT software to run some of the code. Three free suitable downloads of XSLT software are listed in Appendix B, "XML Tools."

To view SVG, you will need an SVG viewer, such as the Adobe SVG Viewer; it can be downloaded free from www.adobe.com/svg/.

To run the code for the DOM and SAX chapters, you will need a JavaScript interpreter (present in almost all Web browsers) and a Java Virtual Machine (already installed on most operating systems).

Source Code and Updates

For updates to this book and to download the source code and examples presented in this book, visit www.samspublishing.com. From the home page, type this book's ISBN (0672324717) into the search window and click Search to access information about the book and for a direct link to the source code.

LESSON 1
What Is XML?

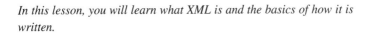

In this lesson, you will learn what XML is and the basics of how it is written.

What Is XML For?

Many newcomers to XML, the Extensible Markup Language, find it difficult to grasp what XML is and what XML is for. Part of the difficulty arises from the fact that XML is pretty abstract, and part is because XML can do many things, not just one. Only after you have explored XML for some time do the parts begin to come together to make sense. In addition, the number of XML language standards, such as XSLT, XPath, SVG, and XML Schema, is potentially intimidating.

XML documents are intended for the storage or exchange of data or information. XML "documents" can be used to store data that you would traditionally store as documents—letters, reports, manuals and so on—or data that you might associate with databases.

Note   In XML, a *document* can be what you would normally think of as a document, but it also might be a complex, highly structured hierarchical data store.

A simple XML document could express a letter with a structure similar to the following code:

```
<?xml version="1.0" ?>
<letter>
 <salutation>Dear John</salutation>
 <paragraph>
 I look forward to meeting you on Saturday morning at the
 agreed location.
 </paragraph>
 <paragraph>
 It will be great to see you again after so many years.
 </paragraph>
 <ending>
 Yours sincerely,
 </ending>
 <signature>
 Janet
 </signature>
</letter>
```

 Note   Element type names are case sensitive in XML, unlike the situation that arises using HTML. This means that an element type named myOrder is a different element from MyOrder or myorder.

Equally, an XML "document" can store data that you might associate as being appropriate for storage in a database-management system. For example, you could use XML to store information for a human resources department using a structure similar to the following:

```
<Employees>
 <Employee>
  <Name>
   <FirstName>John</FirstName>
   <MiddleInitials>Q</MiddleInitials>
   <LastName>Campbell</LastName>
  </Name>
  <EmployeeID>12345</EmployeeID>
```

```
  </Employee>
  <Employee>
   <Name>
    <FirstName>Joan</FirstName>
    <MiddleInitials>D</MiddleInitials>
    <LastName>Dupois</LastName>
   </Name>
   <EmployeeID>01234</EmployeeID>
  </Employee>
</Employees>
```

In addition to being suitable for storing many types of data, XML documents can be used to transmit messages, such as those sent across the Internet. If a single character is corrupted in an XML message, the message remains largely intact because each character is no more than that—a single character. Binary formats might be impossible to interpret if one byte is corrupted.

XML Is Human-Readable

XML is, at least for developers, human-readable. Typically, an XML developer uses *element type names* (informally called tag names) that are meaningful.

The readability of a data store expressed in a format such as this

```
DE239, 0123, 01/12/24, 200.87, 02/01/03
```

is much improved by expressing it like this:

```
<order>
 <OrderNumber>DE239</OrderNumber>
 <CustomerID>0123</CustomerID>
 <OrderDate>01/12/24</OrderDate>
 <OrderAmount>200.87</OrderAmount>
 <DespatchDate>02/01/03</DespatchDate>
</order>
```

This is because someone looking at the information for the first time can quickly gather what the document is about.

> **Tip**   Be sure to use meaningful names for elements in your XML documents. XML doesn't make you use meaningful element type names for elements that you invent, but using meaningful names makes it easier for you to maintain the code and for newcomers to the code to understand the meaning of the documents that you create.

The improvement in readability is bought at the price of increasing file size and, if included in a message, increasing transmission time.

Is XML Usable on the Web?

When XML 1.0 was first finalized in 1998, there was a lot of expectation—at least some of it hype—that XML would be transmitted on the Web as XML. At the time of this writing, this hasn't happened, partly because conventional (HTML) Web browsers have added only limited XML capabilities to the existing HTML functionality. Another factor has been the prolonged delays in completing the W3C recommendations for the XML Linking Language (XLink, completed in mid-2001) and the XML Pointer Language (XPointer, not yet a recommendation at the time of this writing). Using XML as XML on the Web has been unrealistic without functional XML linking (XLink) to link to external documents and fragment identifier (XPointer) technologies to link to specified parts of documents.

In addition, XML has lacked forms capabilities for data collection. At the time of this writing, the W3C XForms specification is two steps from being finalized and will likely be finalized soon after the time this book is published.

After XLink, XPointer, and XForms are finalized, using XML application languages on the Web—including the XML-based Scalable Vector Graphics (SVG) specification for vector graphics—becomes more realistic. New XML-dedicated browsers, such as the X-Smiles browser (see `http://www.x-smiles.org`), are appearing, making all-XML Web sites and browsers potentially viable. Users will decide whether the functionality offered is sufficiently improved to displace HTML's current dominant position.

In the meantime, the practical solution that many have chosen is to store information as XML (or in a relational database-management system that can export XML) and present that XML content after transformation to HTML, which is displayed in the conventional way in a Web browser. XSLT transformations are described in Chapter 10, "XSLT—Creating HTML from XML"; Chapter 11, "XSLT—Transforming XML Structure"; and Chapter 12, "XSLT—Sorting XML."

 Note *Transformation* is the process of selecting desired data in an XML document or data store and either restructuring it as another XML document or producing a non-XML document, such as HTML.

XML Is a Markup Language

As its name suggests, XML is a markup language. Markup is used to convey some information about text or other data. XML has similarities to other markup languages.

Markup may be used to indicate how text is to be presented. In a word-processing program, for example, hidden codes communicate to the word-processor software various settings that are applied to a document but that are not visible. Typically, the codes used in word-processing programs are not easy for a typical user to read or decipher.

The Hypertext Markup Language (HTML) uses angled brackets and tags to convey something about the structure of a document to be presented on the World Wide Web. An h1 tag, for example, indicates a top-level heading. HTML markup typically merges information about the presentation of text content with its meaning. The h1 tag, for example, indicates not only a top-level heading but likely also specifies, according to browser settings, a particular font size, and so on.

Markup may also be used to indicate something about the meaning of the text content. For example, if you wanted to express some information about this book using XML syntax, you could write this:

```
<?xml version="1.0" ?>
<book>
 <title>Sams Teach Yourself XML in 10 Minutes</title>
 <author>Andrew Watt</author>
 <publisher>Sams Publishing</publisher>
</book>
```

The use of meaningful element type names results in a logical structure that is better expressed than when using HTML tags. Notice that the preceding code says nothing about how the information is to be presented.

XML Is a Meta Language

XML differs from markup languages such as HTML because XML can have any number of *element type names* that often are informally called *tag names*. This gives application languages that use XML syntax the functionality to represent data from any subject domain. Because all these XML application languages use the same syntax rules, those languages can be processed using a set of common core software tools that understand XML syntax rules, with custom tools being necessary for fewer aspects of processing. This makes possible efficiencies that facilitate data exchange between users and between applications.

A meta language can be thought of as a set of grammar rules. The application languages that follow the specified set of rules can be thought of as a vocabulary. Broadly, in the natural language domain there are sets of rules that specify how words are used with punctuation and so on. Many Western languages broadly follow similar sets of rules at that level, with uppercase initial letters to start a sentence, periods to complete a sentence, and so on. But the words used in each language, such as in English and French, are very different.

Of course, the syntax rules that apply to XML-based application languages are much more tightly defined and consistent than the situation in the natural language realm, but the principles are similar. Using this single set of XML syntax rules, you—or, often more importantly, the World Wide Web Consortium (W3C)—can define multiple languages that follow XML syntax rules precisely. This facilitates processing of code written in those languages because a generic XML processor (also called an XML parser) can parse the characters of files written in that language and can extract its logical structure and pass that logical information to another application more specific to the needs of the application language.

You Can Create Your Own Vocabulary

XML 1.0 is a set of syntax rules. You can create your own set of element type names, as you learned in the short examples earlier in this chapter.

Already the W3C has published specifications for many application languages of XML, including languages to describe the transformation of XML (XSLT, the Extensible Stylesheet Language Transformations, described in Chapters 10–12), to create links among XML documents (the XML Linking Language, XLink, described in Chapter 14, "Linking in XML—XLink"), and to describe vector graphics (SVG, Scalable Vector Graphics).

The syntax rules of XML can also be used by corporations or business consortia to create XML application languages in various business or technical domains. Many business and technical domains have already created common vocabularies to assist data exchange. Common vocabularies use schemas to define the allowed content and structure of a class of XML documents. Schemas can be written using non-XML syntax—Document Type Definitions, described in Chapter 4, "Valid XML—Document Type Definitions"—or using XML syntax, the W3C XML Schema language described in Chapter 19, "Beyond DTDs—W3C XML Schema."

This enormous flexibility of XML needs some order applied to it—after all, if everyone used element type names just as they personally wanted, individuals or companies would use different element type names to describe the same thing or would use the same element type names to describe different concepts. In fact, these problems are pretty much impossible to avoid; this potential for element name clashes led to the development of namespaces in the XML specification. Namespaces are described in Chapter 8, "Namespaces in XML."

How Does XML Relate to HTML?

XML is a meta language, a set of syntax rules. HTML is an application language, a predefined vocabulary that uses the rules of another meta language, Standard Generalized Markup Language (SGML).

Both XML and HTML derive from SGML, but in different ways. XML uses a subset of the syntax rules allowed in SGML documents. In principle, HTML can use all the syntax rules of SGML, but only as a defined vocabulary that makes use of the SGML syntax rules.

HTML has a defined number of tags defined by specification documents produced by W3C. An HTML processor—a Web browser—should process only those tags that are officially approved. With the exception of some legacy or unofficial tags, such as the embed tag, this is what an HTML processor does. XML documents, by contrast, can contain any element names that you choose (subject to the rules for legal characters in XML names, described in Chapter 3, "XML Must Be Well-Formed").

HTML element names are not case sensitive. A Web browser processes a paragraph identically whether it is written as

```
<p>This is a test paragraph</p>
```

or as

```
<P>This is a test paragraph</P>
```

XML, by contrast, *is* case sensitive. For the names of two elements to be treated as identical, each character must match exactly. The Title and title elements in the following code snippet are treated as different elements by an XML processor:

```
<book>
 <Title>Sams Teach Yourself XML in 10 Minutes</Title>
 <author>
  <title>Mr.</title>
  <Name>Andrew Watt</Name>
 </author>
</book>
```

Because the `Title` and `title` elements contain different types of information, it might be desirable to distinguish them. But it is less confusing to choose element type names such as `BookTitle` and `PersonalTitle`.

Separating Content from Presentation

When most Web programming was done on a small scale by individuals, the problems arising from mixing content and presentation existed but weren't a major problem for small-scale HTML users. If you had to make many individual changes, the total number was unlikely to be enormous.

One of the disadvantages of HTML for large projects is that content and presentation are entangled. An `h1` tag indicates that the contained text is a heading, but, depending on the way the browser is configured, it also indicates something about how the text is to be displayed. Increasingly, HTML documents separate presentation from content by using Cascading Style Sheets (CSS).

In XML, by contrast, typically a document describes only the logical structure of the data:

```
<book>
<title>The Bible</title>
<TestamentTitle>The Old Testament</TestamentTitle>
<TestamentTitle>The New Testament</TestamentTitle>
</book>
```

You might expect the text content of the `title` and `TestamentTitle` elements in the preceding code to be displayed as headings, but the XML document contains no information about exactly how they should be presented. Typically, an XML document is styled using CSS style sheets or using XSLT.

 Note   For historical reasons, a CSS style sheet is two words and an XSLT stylesheet is one word.

How Is XML Written?

XML is written using tags. An XML element has a *start tag* that is delimited by angled brackets—written as `<myStartTagName>`—and an *end tag*—written as `</myStartTagName>`—which is also delimited by angled brackets. For example, to create a `title` element in XML, you could write this:

```
<title>Some book title</title>
```

Unlike in some parts of HTML, tags in XML must be used in pairs. Omitting an end tag causes the XML processor to generate an error. Each start tag in XML must have a matching end tag.

> **Note**   An *XML processor* is a piece of software that processes the characters of an XML document and makes available to another piece of software—often called the application—the logical structure of the XML document.

In HTML, you could write this

```
<p>This is a paragraph
<p>This is another paragraph
```

and the Web browser would figure out that the first p tag ends at the end of the first line of code. In HTML, you could also write this to close the tags explicitly:

```
<p>This is a paragraph</p>
<p>This is another paragraph</p>
```

Allowing syntax options in this way makes an HTML processor more complex than if a rule existed that all tags had to be closed.

XML uses that principle to simplify the writing of XML processors. All XML elements must have a matching end tag for each start tag. This means that you must write XML documents correctly or the XML processor will signal an error and stop processing.

If you needed an XML element to describe the title of a book, you could write the title element as follows:

```
<title>Sams Teach Yourself XML in 10 Minutes</title>
<author>Andrew Watt</author>
```

An error would result if you completed the document and did not provide an end tag, `</title>`, to balance the `<title>` start tag.

Adding Attributes to Elements

XML elements often contain qualifying information contained in *attributes*. XML attributes are written inside the start tag of an element, after the element type name and separated from it and any other attributes by whitespace. Finally, optionally, the attribute name/value pair is separated from the closing angled bracket of the start tag by a space character.

Attribute values in XML must be surrounded by paired quotation marks, either a pair of double quotes or apostrophes.

An XML element with one or more attributes could be written like the following code:

```
<Invoice date="2002/12/23">
<InvoiceNumber Dept='ID4'>DA890</InvoiceNumber>
<BillTo>John Smith</BillTo>
<!-- And so on -->
</Invoice>
```

The value of the `date` attribute on the `Invoice` element uses paired double quotes, and the value of the `Dept` attribute is delimited by paired apostrophes. Either paired character is acceptable to an XML processor.

It is an error to omit the paired quotation marks. The following is not legal XML:

```
<Invoice date=2002/12/23>
<!-- And so on -->
</Invoice>
```

Try It Yourself

You have seen how to create simple XML documents that contain elements and attributes. Many XML editors, such as those described in Appendix B, "XML Tools," check that you have written XML documents correctly and help you find errors. Some XML editors with that capability, such as XML Writer (see Appendix B), have a free download that you can try if you want.

Summary

In this lesson, you learned what XML is, what XML can be used for, and how to correctly write XML elements and attributes.

Lesson 2

The Structure of an XML Document

In this lesson you will learn the permitted structure of an XML document and see examples of allowed variations on the basic structure.

An XML Document

An XML document has the following general structure but some parts are optional:

- A *prolog,* which may optionally be empty

- At least one element, the *document element,* although a typical XML document has a nested structure of elements

- Optional content following the end tag of the document element

Each of these permitted parts of an XML document is described in the remaining sections of this chapter.

A minimal XML document can consist of a single *document element,* such as this:

```
<someElementTypeName>The content</someElementTypeName>
```

Typically, XML documents are much more complex and have a nested structure of elements. An XML document that uses more of the allowed structures might look like this:

```
<?xml version="1.0" ?>
<!-- This is an example XML document. -->
<!DOCTYPE book >
<book>
<title>Sams Teach Yourself XML in 10 Minutes</title>
<author>Andrew Watt</author>
</book>
```

First let's look at what can go in the prolog.

Prolog

The *prolog* of an XML document, when present, precedes the *document element*.

The prolog may, but need not, contain the following:

- An XML declaration

- Miscellaneous content—processing instructions or comments

- A Document Type Declaration, also called a DOCTYPE declaration

Let's look at each of these in turn.

The XML Declaration

The XML declaration can be as simple as this:

```
<?xml version="1.0" ?>
```

This declaration is an optional part of all XML documents. However, when an XML declaration is present in an XML document, it must occur in the first line of the XML document and must have no characters—not even a single space character—before it.

An XML declaration, if present, must have a version attribute. For XML documents that correspond to version 1.0 of XML, the only permitted value for the `version` attribute is `1.0`. Future versions of XML might use different version numbers, allowing XML processors to process only versions of XML that they recognize.

> **Note**   At the time of this writing, only a value of `1.0` is meaningful. However, version 1.1 of XML is currently in draft at the W3C.

Optionally, an XML declaration may include an `encoding` attribute. When present, this attribute indicates the character encoding being used in the document. All XML processors must be capable of processing XML documents encoded in the UTF-8 and UTF-16 character encodings. So, if an XML document is encoded in UTF-8 or UTF-16, no encoding attribute is needed because all conforming XML processors will be capable of processing the document. Optionally, XML processors may choose to support additional character encodings. When using other encodings, it is advisable to specify an `encoding` attribute and the appropriate value. Character encoding is discussed further in Chapter 6, "Characters in XML."

> **Note**   Strictly speaking, an XML declaration is not a processing instruction, although the initial delimiter, `<?`, and the closing delimiter, `?>`, are the same as those used by processing instructions. These are described in the following section.

The XML declaration may also include a `standalone` attribute. The `standalone` attribute takes the values of `yes` or `no`. If external *markup declarations* supply default values for attributes or if entities (other than built-in entities—see Chapter 5, "XML Entities") are declared, the `standalone` attribute must have the value of `no`.

> **Note**   A *markup declaration* declares the existence of, for example, an element or attribute in the relevant class of XML documents. It defines permitted or default values in some circumstances.

Comments and Processing Instructions

XML documents may contain comments, which contain information intended for human consumption or processing instructions.

> **Note**   XML comments and processing instructions described in the following sections may occur in the prolog, within the document element, and after the end tag of the document element.

XML Comments

XML comments may occur anywhere outside other markup. In other words, comments cannot be used within the start or end tags of elements, within processing instructions, or within entity references, empty element tags, character references, CDATA section delimiters, Document Type Declarations, XML declarations or text declarations. Any unfamiliar terms are explained in more detail later.

XML comments use the same syntax as HTML comments:

```
<!-- This is an XML comment -->
```

The character sequence <!-- is the starting delimiter of an XML comment, and the character sequence --> is the ending delimiter. The text contained between these delimiters can contain any characters (with exceptions described in the next paragraph), including those that must be escaped when present within element or attribute values (such as the left angle bracket or right angle bracket). Implicitly, the text content of an XML comment is marked as unparsed information and, therefore, need not satisfy the requirements for other parsed content.

For compatibility with SGML, the character string -- must not occur within an XML comment. Also, it is illegal to end an XML comment with the character sequence --->, which has three consecutive dashes.

XML Processing Instructions

An XML document is viewed in the XML 1.0 Recommendation as being parsed by an XML parser that then passes the results of that parsing to an *application*. Sometimes it might be appropriate to pass to the application instructions intended for the use of the application rather than the results of parsing human-readable markup. Because processing instructions are intended for use outside the XML processor, they are not considered part of the character content of the XML document.

An XML processing instruction is delimited by the starting character sequence <? and by the ending character sequence ?>.

An XML processing instruction takes the following general form:

```
<? target characterSequence ?>
```

Here, `target` is any XML name, excluding the character sequence xml or XML, in any combination of upper- or lowercase. The `target` identifies the application to which the `characterSequence` should be passed. The `characterSequence` that constitutes the message to the application must not include the character sequence ?>, otherwise, an XML processor would assume that the processing instruction had been completed.

One common example of the use of a processing instruction is the xml-stylesheet processing instruction used to associate a stylesheet—either XSLT (Extensible Stylesheet Language Transformations) or CSS (Cascading Style Sheet)—with an XML document.

For example, to associate a stylesheet stored in a file called myStylesheet.xsl, you might use the following processing instruction to associate the XSLT stylesheet (introduced in Chapter 10, "XSLT—Creating HTML from XML") with the XML document, assuming that the stylesheet is stored in the same directory as the XML document:

```
<?xml-stylesheet href="myStylesheet.xsl" type="text/xsl"?>
```

Document Type Declaration

The Document Type Declaration, also called the DOCTYPE declaration, is optional. If present, it must occur before the document element. The DOC-TYPE declaration specifies the element type name of the document element and, optionally, references external markup declarations or may include markup declarations.

The simplest form of the Document Type Declaration may be written as follows:

```
<!DOCTYPE theDocumentElement >
<theDocumentElement>
<!-- The content of the document element would go here -->
</theDocumentElement>
```

As written, the preceding DOCTYPE declaration simply indicates that the document element of the XML document has the element type name of theDocumentElement.

In addition to indicating the element type name of the document element, the DOCTYPE declaration contains or points to the markup declarations that optionally define the permitted structure of an XML document. The markup declarations provide a grammar for a class of XML documents.

A DOCTYPE Declaration, when present, may have two additional optional parts:

- An indication of the location of the *external subset* of the Document Type Definition, DTD (see Chapter 4, "Valid XML—Document Type Definitions," for further explanation)

- A set of markup declarations that constitute the *internal subset* of the DTD (also discussed in Chapter 4)

When an external subset of the DTD exists, it may be expressed as a relative URI, as follows:

```
<!DOCTYPE documentElementName SYSTEM "myDTD.dtd" >
```

Here, SYSTEM is a keyword indicating that the location of the external subset of the DTD is specified relative to the current system. The *system identifier*—myDTD.dtd, in this case—is a uniform resource identifier (URI) that indicates the location of the external subset.

A system identifier may be identified by a relative URI, as in the preceding example, or a full URI reference, as follows:

```
<!DOCTYPE myElement SYSTEM "http://www.XMML.com/myDTD.dtd">
```

An alternate syntax is to specify a *public identifier*, using the keyword PUBLIC, together with a system identifier:

```
<!DOCTYPE documentElementName PUBLIC publicidentifier SYSTEM
    myDTD.dtd >
```

This form is used when a public identifier is appropriate—for example, in the DOCTYPE declaration of the XML application language Extensible Hypertext Markup Language (XHTML) documents. For XHTML version 1.0, the DOCTYPE declaration is as follows:

```
<!DOCTYPE html
    PUBLIC "-//W3C//DTD XHTML 1.0 Transitional//EN"
    SYSTEM "http://www.w3.org/TR/xhtml1/DTD/xhtml1-
    transitional.dtd" >
```

The public identifier indicates an organization—in this case, the W3C—and also includes an indication of the language—in this case, English, indicated by EN.

The syntax for defining the internal subset of the DTD is described in Chapter 4.

> **Caution** The Document Type Declaration and the Document Type Definition (DTD) are not identical, although they are closely related. The Document Type Declaration defines the location of the external subset of the DTD and optionally may contain the internal subset of the DTD.

Document Element

Each XML document must have one—and only one—*document element*, which is sometimes referred to as the *root element*.

> **Caution**   Be careful if you use or read the term *root* without any further clarification. The XML 1.0 specification uses the term apparently as a synonym for the document entity (Chapter 2 of the XML 1.0 Recommendation) and also as a synonym for the document element (Chapter 2.1).

Elements Nested Inside the Document Element

Typically, nested within the document element is a hierarchy of other elements, represented as start tag/end tag pairs or as empty element tags.

Elements must be nested correctly. The following code shows a correctly nested pair of elements:

```
<chapter>
 <section number="1">Some content
 </section>
</chapter>
```

The start tag of the section element follows the start tag of the chapter element, so the end tag of the section element must come before the end tag of the chapter element.

When correctly nested as shown in the preceding code, the chapter element is termed the parent element of the section element. The section element is termed the child element of the chapter element. An element may have zero, one, or more child elements. An element may have zero or one parent elements. All elements except the document element have one parent element. The document element does not have a parent element.

The following is not legal XML because the elements are not nested correctly:

```
<chapter>
<section number="1">Some content
</chapter>
</section>
```

Attributes

An element may be qualified by adding attribute name/value pairs to its start tag. An attribute is indicated by an XML name, followed by the equal sign and a pair of either quotation marks or apostrophes. The *value* of the attribute is contained within those quotation marks or apostrophes.

So, if you want to indicate that this is the first edition of this book and that it is published in English, you could add edition and language attributes to the start tag of the book element:

```
<book edition="1" language='English'>
<title>Sams Teach Yourself XML in 10 Minutes</title>
<author>Andrew Watt</author>
<publisher>Sams Publishing</publisher>
</book>
```

The value of the edition attribute is contained in a pair of quotation marks. The value of the language attribute is contained in a pair of apostrophes.

It is an error to mix double quotes and single quotes as the delimiters of an attribute. In the following code, both the edition and language attributes would generate an error from the XML processor because the attribute value delimiters are not correctly paired.

```
<book edition="1' language='English" >
```

CDATA Sections

An XML document may contain information expressed in a non-XML syntax. The XML mechanism for indicating that such content is not to be parsed as XML is the CDATA *section*.

The starting delimiter of a CDATA section is the character sequence
`<![CDATA[`. The ending delimiter is the character sequence `]]>`. The character sequence `]]>` cannot be used as the content of a CDATA section.

CDATA sections can be used to store XML code, such as code snippets used in this book, without having to escape all characters that an XML processor would recognize as markup. For example, if the text of this chapter were written and stored in XML, you would not want example code to be parsed. Thus, if you wanted to create in XML the text for a section of this book that referred to example text expressed as XML, you could write something like this:

```
<example>
<![CDATA[
<book>
<title>Sams Teach Yourself XML in 10 Minutes</title>
<author>Andrew Watt</author>
</book>
]]>
</example>
```

If you didn't use a CDATA section, you would have to write this:

```
<example>
&lt;book&gt;
&lt;title&gt;Sams Teach Yourself XML in 10
   Minutes&lt;/title&gt;
&lt;author&gt;Andrew Watt&lt;/author&gt;
&lt;/book&gt;
</example>
```

It very quickly becomes tedious having to write < for each < character and > for each > character in a section of example code. The CDATA section is more convenient.

One common use of CDATA sections appears in Scalable Vector Graphics (SVG) documents (SVG is an XML application language for two-dimensional graphics), which can contain scripting code written, for example, in JavaScript. The general structure using the SVG script element would look as follows:

```
<script type="text/javascript" >
<![CDATA[

//JavaScript code goes here
]]>
</script>
```

CDATA sections cannot be nested within each other because the starting delimiter <![CDATA[is recognized only as a sequence of characters, not as a starting delimiter of a nested CDATA section. Only the ending delimiter character sequence,]]>, is recognized as markup within a CDATA section.

Text Content

Text, which is basically a sequence of characters, may occur between the start tag and end tag of an element; it is said to be (or to form part of) the element's *content*.

Most English alphabetic or numeric characters can simply be typed as normal. Certain characters must not be used in text content, however. The following simple description of an arithmetic axiom in XML generates an error in an XML processor:

```
<axiom> 1 < 2 </axiom>
```

An XML processor recognizes the less than sign between 1 and 2 as the starting angle bracket of a new tag. An error results upon finding a space and then a number (which is not allowed to start an XML name). The following characters must be escaped to use them in text content:

- < (The less than symbol)—Must be written as <

- > (The greater than symbol)—Must be written as >

- ' (The single quotation mark)—Must be written as '

- " (The double quotation mark)—Must be written as "

- & (The ampersand)— Must be written as &

The alternative is to use these characters written literally (that is, not escaped) within a CDATA section. The choice of whether to escape characters or to enclose them inside a CDATA section often depends on how many characters in a particular section of text require escaping. The more characters need escaping, the more likely it is that using a CDATA section offers the most convenient solution.

Content After the Document Element End Tag

The XML 1.0 specification allows content to follow the end tag of the document element. However, permitted content is restricted to only comments, processing instructions, and whitespace. In practice, this means that all document content must be nested within the document element. Markup after the end tag of the document element can contain only information intended for a human reader, given in comments, or one or more processing instructions for the XML processor or the application. No constraint affects the ordering of comments or processing instructions.

Summary

In this lesson, you learned about the structure of an XML document and saw examples of how to write the most common parts of that structure.

LESSON 3
XML Must Be Well-Formed

In this chapter you will learn the rules that an XML document must satisfy to be considered well-formed.

Well-Formed XML Documents

If XML is to be used as a format for data interchange, it must adhere to a consistent syntax so that programs can reliably produce and parse XML documents. An XML document that adheres to proper XML syntax is said to be well-formed.

If the results of parsing are to be presented by an XML processor (also known as an XML parser) to its associated application, the XML document must be *well-formed*. If the document is not well-formed, the XML processor should report one or more errors encountered, and normal processing, including the passing of parsed data to the application, should stop. Ensuring that the XML documents that you write are well-formed is crucial to achieving the desired processing of the data that they contain.

Some of the rules for well-formedness are straightforward. Some can seem pretty obscure the first time you read them, so if some of the rules in this chapter don't make too much sense the first time through, don't worry too much. As you learn more about other aspects of XML in later chapters, the pieces of the syntax jigsaw will fit together more clearly.

In Chapter 2, "The Structure of an XML Document," you learned about the structure that an XML document must conform to. All well-formed XML documents must follow the permitted options of that structure. In addition to those rules, an XML document must satisfy several other rules to be considered well-formed.

> **Note**   This chapter gives a complete description of
> well-formedness constraints. To do so, it is necessary
> to refer to concepts described more fully in later chap-
> ters. You might find it helpful to reread parts of this
> chapter after reading Chapter 4, "Valid XML—
> Document Type Definitions," and Chapter 5, "XML
> Entities."

The term *well-formed* is used to describe the rules that all XML documents must satisfy. If an XML document is not well-formed, an XML
processor signals an error and stops normal processing. It is crucial that
you understand the well-formedness constraints in XML 1.0, to ensure
that the XML documents that you create will be processed correctly and
without errors.

To be well-formed, an XML document must satisfy each of three broad
rules or sets of rules:

- The structure of the document must follow that described in
  Chapter 2—an optional prolog, followed by a required document
  element (and any content that it has) and, finally, an optional
  miscellaneous section.

- The document must satisfy the well-formedness constraints
  described in the following sections of this chapter.

- Any parsed entities referenced from the document, whether
  directly or indirectly, must themselves be well-formed.

The following several sections consider each of the XML 1.0 well-
formedness constraints.

XML Names

The XML 1.0 Recommendation places restrictions on the characters that
may be used in legal XML names and imposes tighter restrictions on the
characters that may be used as the first character in an XML name.

Initial Characters of XML Names

In English, the initial character of an XML name must be either a letter (from A to Z—both upper- and lowercase are legal), the colon character (:), or the underscore character (_).

 Tip   Avoid the colon character as the first character in an XML name. Using that character is legal but could cause confusion when you create XML documents using elements from several XML namespaces (described in Chapter 8, "Namespaces in XML").

XML is case sensitive, so the following two elements are considered in XML to be different elements because of the difference in case:

```
<p></p>
```

```
<P></P>
```

In some other languages, ideographic characters may also be used as the initial character of an XML name.

It is illegal to start an XML name with a numeric character. The following code generates an error because 2d is not a legal XML name:

```
<?xml version='1.0'?>
<myElement>
 <2d>
  Some content.
 </2d>
</myElement>
```

Caution   Names in XML 1.0 must not begin with the character sequence xml or XML, in any combination of upper- or lowercase.

All characters that are legal as the first character of an XML name can be used in later positions within an XML name as well.

Non-Initial Characters of XML Names

The non-initial characters of an XML name are allowed to include characters not permitted as the first character of an XML name. The additional allowed characters are numeric characters from 0 to 9 inclusive, the hyphen character, and the period character.

> **Tip** Again, avoid using the colon character later in XML names. Later you will want to mix XML documents from different namespaces (discussed in Chapter 8), and the colon character has special meaning in those circumstances. Avoiding the colon character except in namespace-aware documents means that you won't have to change your documents if you want to use multiple namespaces later.

Elements

XML elements must have as their element type name a legal XML name as defined in the preceding section.

Additionally, the element type name in the start tag must match the element type name in the end tag. It is important to remember that XML is case sensitive. Any of the following tag pairs will generate well-formedness errors because of case differences:

```
<title></TITLE>
```

```
<title></Title>
```

```
<title></Title>
```

Balanced Start and End Tags

Each start tag must have a corresponding end tag, properly nested. The following example is correctly nested:

```
<oneElement>Some text
 <anotherElement>Some other text
 </anotherElement>
<oneElement>
```

The end tag of the `anotherElement` element must appear before the end tag of the `oneElement` element.

If an element is empty (that is, it has no content, not even a single white-space character), the start tag/end tag pair can be written as an empty element tag. The following

```
<someElement myAttribute="someInformation"></someElement>
```

is equivalent to writing this:

```
<someElement myAttribute="someInformation"/>
```

Attributes

An attribute is the association of an attribute name with an attribute value. For example, the markup describing this book might be represented as follows:

```
<book edition="1">
<title>Sams Teach Yourself XML in 10 Minutes</title>
</book>
```

The `book` element has an `edition` attribute, which has the value of 1.

An attribute is allowed only in the start tag of an element. The value of an attribute must be enclosed between paired double quotation marks, such as

```
<book edition="1">
```

or between paired apostrophes:

```
<book edition='1'>
```

It is an error to mix these two types of delimiters. The next two line of code would cause a well-formedness error because the delimiters of the attribute value are not paired.

In the following line, the quotation mark before the attribute value is not paired with a matching quotation mark:

```
<book edition="1'>
```

Here, the apostrophe before the attribute value does not have a matching apostrophe to delimit the end of the attribute value:

```
<book edition='1">
```

Attributes Must Be Unique

The start tag of any XML element must not contain duplicate attribute names.

For example, the following code will generate an error because there are two number attributes in the start tag of the chapter element.

```
<chapter number="1" author="DPT" number='1'>
<!-- Some text would go here -->
</chapter>
```

No External Entity References

Attribute values are not allowed to contain external entity references.

For example, imagine that you had declared an external entity called copyright:

```
<!ENTITY copyright SYSTEM "copyright.xml">
```

You could not use it in an attribute value, such as in the following code:

```
<book status="&copyright;">
<!-- Content goes here -->
</book>
```

However, attribute values are allowed to contain references to internal parsed entities.

For example, imagine that the internal subset of the DTD included an entity declaration as follows:

```
<!ENTITY BigText "font-size:72">
```

It could be used to define the style of text nested in an SVG text element, as follows:

```
<text style="&BigText;">This text is big!!</text>
```

No < in Attribute Values

The value of an XML attribute is not allowed to include the < character, either directly or indirectly.

It is not legal to write this:

```
<math comparison="3<4"></math>
```

It is also an error to include an internal entity reference to an entity, such as

```
<!ENTITY lessthan "3<4">
```

which is referenced like this:

```
<math comparison="&lessthan;"></math>
```

After the entity reference was replaced by its replacement text, it would result in the same illegal code:

```
<math comparison="3<4"></math>
```

Following the well-formedness constraints described for elements and attributes in the preceding sections will help you avoid many of the common well-formedness errors. As your documents become more complex, other well-formedness constraints might become important.

Other Characteristics of Well-Formedness

This section covers the well-formedness constraints as they apply to areas other than elements and attributes. Several of the well-formedness rules will make more sense after you have read Chapters 4 and 5.

Comments

To be well formed, XML comments must not end with the character sequence ‑‑‑>. A legal XML comment ends with ‑‑>— that is, two dashes and a greater than character.

Entities Must Be Declared

If a reference to an entity is present in an XML document and any of the following are true, any entity referenced must be declared:

- There is no Document Type Definition (DTD).

- A document has only an internal DTD subset with no parameter entity references.

- The value of the standalone attribute in the XML declaration is yes.

The exception to this rule is that the built-in entities amp, apos, gt, lt, and quot need not be declared.

External Parsed Entities

External parsed entities must be well-formed. They optionally begin with a *text declaration* (described more fully in Chapter 5). A text declaration is similar to an XML declaration but may have only version and encoding attributes. A text declaration does not have a standalone attribute. Following the text declaration, the structure need not all be contained in a single element—the document element is contained in the XML document entity that references the external parsed entity.

The allowed content is any combination of the following:

- Character data

- Elements

- Entity references

- Character references

- CDATA sections

- Processing instructions

- Comments

The content following the text declaration is essentially the same as the permitted content of an element anywhere in the document entity. That is not surprising because an external parsed entity can have replacement text that constitutes the content of an element in the document entity.

An internal parsed entity is well-formed if the replacement text matches the content that was listed in the preceding list.

No element or other markup may begin in one external entity and end in another.

Parsed Entities: No Recursion

Entities are discussed in more detail in Chapter 5. A parsed entity is not permitted to directly or indirectly reference itself.

Parameter Entity References in the DTD

Parameter entity references may appear only in the DTD.

Parameter Entity References in Internal Subset

Parameter entity references in the internal subset of the DTD, which is described more fully in Chapter 4, can occur only where markup declarations can occur and not within other markup declarations.

External Subset of the DTD

The external subset of the DTD may have the following structure. It may optionally begin with a text declaration (described in Chapter 5) and may also contain markup declarations or conditional sections (both described in Chapter 4).

Two separators are allowed between markup declarations, parameter entities and whitespace.

Parameter Entities in Markup Declarations

A parameter entity has replacement text. The replacement text of a parameter entity must satisfy the constraints on declarations, as described in the preceding section, so that the replacement text nests properly.

Replacement Text

When an entity reference appears in an attribute value or a parameter entity appears in an entity declaration, the replacement text might contain either a double quotation mark or an apostrophe. In this situation, when the double quotation mark or the apostrophe is applied as replacement text, it is treated as a literal character of the relevant type, not the closing delimiter of the attribute value.

For example, with the entity declaration

```
<!ENTITY myEntity "something with an apostrophe'">
```

this entity reference is well-formed:

```
<someElement someAttribute='&myEntity' />
```

The same is true with a parameter entity such as this one:

```
<!ENTITY % hisStatement  '"I agree."'>
<!ENTITY aSentence "He said, &hisStatement;">
```

The replacement text for the hisStatement parameter entity contains two double quotation marks, the first of which would normally be the closing delimiter of the replacement text of the aSentence entity. However, both double quotation marks contained in the parameter reference are treated literally, not as the closing delimiter.

Character References

In XML documents, a character may be referenced using a character reference. You might want to use a character reference when, for example, a character cannot be typed from the keyboard. A character reference beginning with &x# indicates a hexadecimal reference to a character's code point. For example, the uppercase A may be written as the character reference, &x#0041;.

```
<?xml version='1.0'?>
<capitalA>&#x0041;</capitalA>
```

Character references can also be expressed using the &# syntax, indicating a decimal reference to a character's code point. Using this syntax, you can represent the uppercase A as A, as shown here:

```
<capitalA>&#0065;</capitalA>
```

Declaring Predefined Entities

If compatibility with SGML is not an issue in your use of XML, this well-formedness constraint can perhaps be ignored. However, it might help you understand what at first sight could appear to be strange entity declarations in XML documents created by others.

All XML processors must recognize the entities amp, apos, gt, lt, and quot, whether they are explicitly declared or not. However, if compatibility with SGML is a relevant issue, these predefined entities must be explicitly declared in the internal subset of the DTD.

You might recall that you cannot use the literal characters &, ', >, <, and " in well-formed character data without causing a well-formedness error. Therefore, you cannot use any of these characters literally as the replacement text of an entity declaration. The solution is to use character references for each of the characters.

Therefore, entity declarations used for compatibility with SGML can be written as follows:

```
<!ENTITY amp "&#x26; &#38">
<!ENTITY apos "&#x27; &#39">
<!ENTITY gt "&#x3E; &#62">
<!ENTITY lt "&#x3C; &#60">
<!ENTITY quot "&#x22; &#34">
```

Well-Formedness and XML Processor Type

XML processors can be viewed as being of two types, validating processors and nonvalidating processors. Validation is discussed further in Chapter 4.

Both validating processors and nonvalidating processors detect any well-formedness errors in the document entity, including the internal subset of the DTD. However, their behavior might differ with external entities and the external subset of the DTD.

A validating processor must process the XML document entity, any external entities, and the DTD (both internal subset and external subset). It must access those fully to validate the XML document. In doing so, it detects any well-formedness errors in any physical part of an XML document.

Nonvalidating processors, on the other hand, need not access an external subset of the DTD (if it exists) or external entities. So, well-formedness errors might not be detected by nonvalidating processors if the well-formedness errors occur outside the document entity itself.

Another potential source of confusion with nonvalidating processors is that although they are not obliged to access parts of the document other than the document entity, nothing in the XML specification prevents them doing so. Therefore, one nonvalidating processor might detect errors that another nonvalidating processor misses because the former processor accessed external entities that the latter ignored. This could be confusing if you find no errors in your code but a recipient of a document that you have written finds errors. The recipient might simply be using a nonvalidating processor that checks more parts of the document than the nonvalidating processor that you used to run the code.

Summary

In this lesson, you learned all the XML 1.0 well-formedness constraints. Those relating to elements and attributes likely will be most directly relevant to straightforward XML documents. Other well-formedness constraints less likely will be directly useful to simple code. However, you might find that knowing these constraints helps you write code that runs correctly.

LESSON 4

Valid XML— Document Type Definitions

In this lesson, you will learn what valid XML documents are, why document type definitions for XML documents are needed, and how to write a DTD for XML documents.

Shared Documents: Why We Need DTDs

The well-formedness rules examined in Chapter 2, "The Structure of an XML Document," and Chapter 3, "XML Must Be Well-Formed," either ensure that XML processors handle XML documents that satisfy XML's syntax rules or signal an error indicating that the document isn't suitable for further processing. For some purposes, that is sufficient.

For many purposes, particularly when documents are being shared among business partners, for example, it is useful for XML documents also to conform to a known, predictable structure. Of course, it is possible to write custom code in Java or some other programming language to make appropriate checks of a received document's structure. However, it is potentially more convenient to check structure using the validation tools that form part of a validating XML processor.

In XML, a document type definition (DTD) defines the allowed structure of a class of XML documents. A validating XML processor can use the DTD to confirm that a document conforms to the relevant DTD. Using XML-based validation cuts down on the need to write custom code.

> **Note**   Two broad types of XML processor exist. A *nonvalidating XML processor* checks that documents conform to the rules of XML syntax, but it doesn't check for any specific structure of elements or attributes. A *validating XML processor* checks for well-formedness and also checks that the document conforms to a defined structure.

XML documents are ideal for sharing information using a standard syntax. The recipient of information expressed in XML might want to check that the structure of the information received corresponds to what he expects. If the structure of the received information can be checked automatically rather than by writing customized code, this is significantly more efficient.

Document Structure Is Defined in a DTD

The only schema mechanism provided in the XML 1.0 Recommendation is the document type definition (DTD).

> **Note**   A *schema* is a document that defines the allowed structure, or its variants, of a *class* of XML documents. Schemas for XML 1.0 documents may be written in non-XML syntax, a DTD, or, more recently in XML syntax, using a variety of schema languages. For example, the W3C XML Schema is described in Chapter 19, "Beyond DTDs—W3C XML Schema."

A DTD contains markup declarations in two subsets, the *internal subset* and the *external subset*. Taken together, these define the allowed structure of a class of XML documents.

Typically, a group of companies or other organizations with a common interest in a particular type of information will agree (after sometimes lengthy discussion) to automate important processes. That will generate a list of documents that they want to exchange and, in turn, agree on a common structure to be used for the exchange of certain types of business or technical information. The formal expression of the agreed-upon structure is a DTD or other type of schema.

What Is a Valid XML Document?

An XML document that contains a DOCTYPE declaration and that complies with the constraints for that class of XML document expressed in the document type declaration is said to be *valid*. In other words, a valid XML document must comply with a defined logical structure.

All valid XML documents must be well-formed and must satisfy the well-formedness constraints described in Chapter 3. Some well-formed XML documents lack a DOCTYPE declaration and cannot be valid; others might have a DOCTYPE declaration but not comply fully with its constraints. Those documents are not valid XML, either.

What a DTD Is

A DTD is a description of the allowed structure of a class of XML documents.

In a DTD, you *declare* elements, attributes, and so on that are allowed in the structure of a corresponding class of XML documents. Elements and other parts of an XML document are declared in *markup declarations*.

The following are the types of markup declaration in XML 1.0:

- Element declarations
- Attribute list declarations

- Entity declarations

- Notation declarations

Markup declarations may be contained in part or entirely within parameter entities.

The DTD Is Not the **DOCTYPE** Declaration

Earlier, when defining a valid document, this chapter indicated that a valid document complies with the constraints expressed in the DOCTYPE declaration.

It is important to be clear about the differences between the document type *definition*, the DTD, and the document type *declaration* (also called the DOCTYPE declaration). They are not the same, although they are closely related.

The document type declaration contains or refers to information about the permitted structure of an XML document. In other words, the document type declaration may contain part of the DTD, refer to the location of part of the DTD, or do both. The DTD can be spread across two subsets: the *external subset* and the *internal subset*. Either subset may be empty in any particular situation, or both subsets may contain markup declarations. If markup declarations are present in the external subset and include default values for attributes, the standalone attribute in the XML declaration of an *instance XML document* must have the value no.

 Note   An *instance document* is a document that conforms to the defined structure for the class of XML documents to which it belongs.

The External Subset

The external subset of the DTD typically exists as a separate file with a file extension of .dtd.

For example, this short XML document

```
<?xml version="1.0" ?>
<!DOCTYPE book SYSTEM "book.dtd">
<book>
<title>1984</title>
<author>George Orwell</author>
</book>
```

would have a DTD contained in a file, book.dtd, with the following structure:

```
<!ELEMENT book (title,author) >
<!ELEMENT title (#PCDATA) >
<!ELEMENT author (#PCDATA) >
```

That would be contained in the same directory as the XML document.

> **Note** The character content of elements is termed
> PCDATA, meaning parsed character data. The character
> content of attributes is termed CDATA, meaning
> character data.

The Internal Subset

The internal subset of the DTD is contained within the DOCTYPE declaration. The opening delimiter of the internal subset is the [character, and the closing delimiter is the] character.

To incorporate the markup declarations in an internal subset, the XML document would be rewritten as this:

```
<?xml version="1.0" ?>
<!DOCTYPE book [
<!ELEMENT book (title,author) >
<!ELEMENT title (#PCDATA) >
<!ELEMENT author (#PCDATA) >
]>
<book>
<title>1984</title>
<author>George Orwell</author>
</book>
```

The internal subset, if it exists for a particular document, is contained within the DOCTYPE declaration. The start of the internal subset is indicated by a square bracket character, [, and the end of the internal subset is indicated by the corresponding square bracket character,]. The DOCTYPE declaration is then closed by a right angle bracket, >.

Conditional Sections

A DTD may contain *conditional sections*. Conditional sections can be used to control when to use or ignore single markup declarations or a list of markup declarations.

Two options exist: INCLUDE (the default) and IGNORE:

```
<!INCLUDE[
oneOrMoreMarkupDeclarations
]>
```

or

```
<!IGNORE[
oneOrMoreMarkupDeclarations
]>
```

Conditional sections can be used with parameter entities, which are described more fully in Chapter 5, "XML Entities."

Declaring Elements in DTDs

Defining the structure of an XML document must always involve the declaration of elements because all XML documents contain at least one element: the document element.

An element declaration takes this general form:

```
<!ELEMENT elementTypeName contentModel >
```

The allowed content models are listed here:

- Text only—Indicated by (#PCDATA). No element content is allowed.
- Empty element—Indicated by EMPTY. Not even whitespace is allowed as content.

- Any content—Indicated by ANY. Any well-formed content is allowed.

- Mixed content—Indicated by MIXED. This allows text content to be mixed with element content declared in the element declaration.

- Child elements—Indicated by one or more element names contained in parentheses, with any appropriate cardinality indicators.

Consider a simple XML document, such as the following:

```
<simpleMessage>
Here is a simple message.
</simpleMessage>
```

The following element declaration could be used to indicate that the simpleMessage element may contain only parsed character data, indicated by #PCDATA in the element declaration.

```
<!ELEMENT simpleMessage (#PCDATA) >
```

The simpleMessage element is constrained to contain parsed character data only. The presence of any elements in the content of the simpleMessage element would render that instance document invalid.

Typically, you would want to allow element content within a document element. To do so, you must declare the allowed elements. Consider an instance document with the following structure:

```
<book>
<title>Sams Teach Yourself XML in 10 Minutes</title>
<author>Andrew Watt</author>
<publisher>Sams Publishing</publisher>
</book>
```

You could indicate that a book element is allowed to contain a title element, an author element, and a publisher element, in that order, as follows:

```
<!ELEMENT book (title, author, publisher) >
```

You have not yet defined the allowed content of the `title`, `author`, and `publisher` elements—in this case, each has parsed character data. You would do so by completing the DTD as follows:

```
<!ELEMENT book (title, author, publisher) >
<!ELEMENT title (#PCDATA) >
<!ELEMENT author (#PCDATA) >
<!ELEMENT publisher (#PCDATA) >
```

The preceding DTD indicates that the `book` element is the document element. It may contain one and exactly one `title` element, followed by a single `author` element, then followed by a single `publisher` element.

In many settings, an element has more than one child element of a particular element type. Thus, you need ways to express the allowed frequency of occurrence—the cardinality—of child elements.

Cardinality

In XML 1.0, the default cardinality is exactly one occurrence of, for example, an element. Therefore, the absence of any of the cardinality operators in the following list indicates that an element is allowed to occur exactly once.

In addition, the DTD can express three choices of cardinality that must be explicitly expressed within markup declarations:

- Optional, but may only occur once at most—Zero or one occurrences. This is indicated by the ? character.

- Optional, but may occur many times—A minimum of zero occurrences and an unlimited maximum. This is indicated by the * character.

- Required, but may occur many times—A minimum of one occurrence and an unlimited maximum. This is indicated by the + character.

> **Note** A DTD cannot express the notion that an element must occur, say, a minimum of 3 times and a maximum of 20 times.

For example, consider a customer order with a structure similar to the following:

```
<order>
<date>
2003/04/01
</date>
<customerID>
AB987
</customerID>
<items>
<item productID="1234" quantity="10">
3.5" floppy disks
</item>
<item productID="2345" quantity="20">
Write once CDROMs
</item>
</items>
<customerComment>I need the floppy disks as soon as possible.
</customerComment>
<customerComment>
Don't attempt delivery on a Friday.
</customerComment>
</order>
```

You could express that using the following markup declarations:

```
<!ELEMENT order (date, customerID, items, customerComment*) >
<!ELEMENT date (#PCDATA)>
<!ELEMENT customerID (#PCDATA) >
<!ELEMENT items (item)+ >
<!ELEMENT customerComment (#PCDATA) >
<!ELEMENT item (#PCDATA) >
<!ATTLIST item
 productID CDATA #REQUIRED
 quantity CDATA #REQUIRED>
```

In the first line of the code, the date, customerID, and items elements are declared without any cardinality operator. They are required and can occur only once. The customerComment element is declared with a * cardinality operator, indicating that it is optional but can occur more than once.

The declaration of the items element specifies that there must be at least one item element as its child, but that the item element may occur more than once.

Declaring Attributes in DTDs

An XML element in a well-formed document may not have two attributes of the same name. Therefore, cardinality operators are not required when attributes are declared.

The declaration of attributes takes the following general form:

```
<!ATTLIST
 attributeName attributeType defaultDeclaration
>
```

The *attributeType* is any of the values in the following list:

- CDATA—Any legal XML string.

- ENTITY—Value that must match the name of an external unparsed entity.

- ENTITIES—An ENTITY, except that more than one whitespace-separated name may occur.

- ID—Value that must begin with a letter and then must consist of letters, numeric characters, hyphens, underscores, and period characters. At most, one attribute on any element can be of type ID. An ID attribute value must be unique in the XML document.

- IDREF—The value of the attribute must match the value of an ID attribute elsewhere in the same XML document.

- IDREFS—An IDREF, except that it may match more than one ID attribute value elsewhere in an XML document.

- NMTOKEN—The attribute value may contain only letters, numeric characters, and colons. No whitespace is allowed.

- NMTOKENS—An NMTOKEN, except that multiple values that do not contain whitespace are separated by whitespace characters.

The *defaultDeclaration* indicates whether a value is required, is optional, is fixed, or has a default value:

- #FIXED "*someValueInQuotes*"—The value of the attribute is fixed to the value given inside the quotation marks.

- #IMPLIED—A value for the attribute is optional.

- #REQUIRED—A value for the attribute is required.

- "*someValueInQuotes*"—A value for the attribute is optional. If no value is specified for the attribute in the XML document, the value "*someValueInQuotes*" is applied as a default.

For example, suppose that you have a very short XML document, as follows:

```
<order date="2002/11/30" orderNumber="NOV123"
customerID="DB998">
<items>
<!-- And so on -->
</items>
<order>
```

This example shows three attributes of the order element; for business purposes, each of these is essential. These are declared as a list of attributes associated with the order element. The ATTLIST keyword implies an attribute list, but you can define as few as one attribute.

```
<!ELEMENT order (items)>
<!-- An element declaration for the items element would go
   here -->
<!ATTLIST order
customerID CDATA #REQUIRED
date CDATA #REQUIRED
orderNumber CDATA #REQUIRED
>
```

Types of Attributes

XML 1.0 DTDs provide very limited typing of attribute values, as discussed in the preceding section. For data-centric XML documents, this might be insufficient. This is one of the reasons behind the development of W3C XML Schema, described in Chapter 19.

Specifying Default Attribute Values

You can specify default values for attributes when no value is given. For example, consider a business document structured as follows:

```
<Report>
<Paragraph status="public">Some text.</Paragraph>
<Paragraph status="confidential">Some confidential
    text</Paragraph>
<Paragraph>Some text.</Paragraph>
</Report>
```

To preserve confidentiality, you can make it essential that a human actually decide to make any information public by having the following attribute declaration:

```
<!ATTLIST Paragraph status "confidential" #REQUIRED>
```

If an author specifies status="public", the default value is not applied. However, if the author overlooks the need to assign a status attribute to a Paragraph element, the Paragraph element's content is confidential until a human author overrides the default.

Declaring Entities in the DTD

Entities may also be declared in a DTD. This is described in Chapter 5, where entities are discussed in more detail.

Summary

The benefits of sharing XML documents with a predictable structure were discussed in this chapter. You also learned about the concept of a *valid* XML document and gained insight into the use of a Document Type Definition, internal subsets and external subsets, and the correct way to express *markup declarations* for the declaration of elements and attribute lists.

LESSON 5
XML Entities

In this chapter, you will learn about XML entities, what they are, and how you can use them.

What Is an Entity?

An entity is an expression of the physical, rather than logical, structure of an XML document. An entity is a physical data object. When your XML documents are short and simple, you likely will seldom use entities other than the built-in entities. As you begin to create XML documents of greater length and complexity, the usefulness of entities will become more apparent.

One situation in which entities are sometimes used in relatively short documents is in Scalable Vector Graphics (SVG), an XML application language that you will meet in Chapter 15, "Presenting XML Graphically—SVG." In SVG, for example, an entity can be used to define a particular style. If you had an entity called BlackAndRed, you could declare it like this:

```
<!ENTITY BlackAndRed "fill:black;stroke:red">
```

Then you could reuse the entity many times in attribute values in the document, like this:

```
<rect style="&BlackAndRed;" .... />
```

Even when creating the simplest XML documents, you are using at least one entity, although you might not be aware of it. Each XML document has at least one physical entity: the document entity.

An XML document can be viewed as being contained within the document entity. The document entity is not expressed within the syntax of an XML document; instead, it is the container for the syntax that makes up the document.

> **Note**   Most XML entities have a *name*, which is used to reference the entity. The exceptions are the document entity and the external subset of the DTD; these have no name, although both have filenames.

For example, the description of this book used in earlier examples has one logical structure but could be expressed by either of the physical structures shown in the following examples. The simplest expression of the logical structure exists in a single document entity with the description contained in one XML file with the following content, as shown in Listing 5.1.

LISTING 5.1   SingleEntity.xml: A Description of This Book in a Single Document Entity

```
<?xml version="1.0" ?>
<book>
<title>Sams Teach Yourself XML in 10 Minutes</title>
<author>Andrew Watt </author>
<publisher>Sams Publishing</publisher>
</book>
```

Alternatively, the same logical structure could be expressed in several different physical structures. One possibility is to use an external parsed entity to express title information, as in Listing 5.2. For a document as simple as this, there is little practical point in splitting it this way, but the example serves to illustrate the principle.

LISTING 5.2   SplitEntities.xml: A Description of the Book
with an External Parsed Entity

```
<?xml version="1.0" ?>
<!DOCTYPE book [
<!ENTITY bookTitle SYSTEM "title.xml">
]>
<book>
<title>&bookTitle;</title>
<author>Andrew Watt</author>
<publisher>Sams Publishing</publisher>
</book>
```

The file title.xml specified in the entity declaration is shown in Listing
5.3. In a typical external parsed entity in real-life use, the content would
be much more extensive.

LISTING 5.3   Title.xml: A Brief External Entity Referenced in
Listing 5.2

```
Sams Teach Yourself XML in 10 Minutes
```

In Listing 5.2 the entity reference &bookTitle; is used by the XML
processor together with the corresponding entity declaration to find the
file Title.xml and to insert the content of that file between the start tag and
end tag of the title element in Listing 5.2:

```
<!ENTITY bookTitle SYSTEM "title.xml">
```

So, after the external parsed entity has been retrieved, the title element is
processed as if it read as follows:

```
<title>Sams Teach Yourself XML in 10 Minutes</title>
```

 Caution   If the parsed entity is defined in the external subset of the DTD, some nonvalidating XML
parsers might not retrieve external entity declarations.

One use of external entities is to centralize frequently referenced information used by multiple files. In lengthy, complex XML documents, it can be very useful to split documents into entities. For example, a change made in an external parsed entity can be reflected at each place where the entity reference occurs in the XML document and other documents that reference the same external parsed entity.

You might structure financial results using separate XML files for each quarter's figures. For example, the sales figures for Quarter 1 2003 might be represented as follows:

```
<Q12003>
 <Total Sales>$74,300,000</TotalSales>
 <GrossProfit>$2,900,000</GrossProfit>
 <NetProfit>$1,500,000</NetProfit>
</Q12003>
```

If you stored that content in a file named Q12003.xml, you could reference that data in several places after declaring an entity:

```
<!ENTITY Q12003Sales system "Q12003.xml">
```

It makes sense to store the data once rather than risk it being stored in several places with inconsistent data. If that data was referenced several times, such as in department reports and company reports, it would make sense to store it once and then reference it each time it is used.

Entities and Entity References

An entity is a data object. An *entity reference* refers to a parsed entity or parameter entity. The entity referenced may be either a *parsed entity* or a *parameter entity*. The syntax for referencing these two types of entities differs.

> **Note**   A parsed entity can be *internal*—declared in the document entity—or *external*—contained in a file (entity) physically separate from the document entity. A parameter entity is declared and referenced within the DTD, in either the internal or the external subset.

Parsed entities are referenced by an initial & character followed immediately by the entity's name and a semicolon. If you had declared an internal parsed entity called myEntity

```
<!ENTITY myEntity "This is my own entity">
```

you would reference it as follows:

&myEntity;

You can, of course, choose any name that makes sense in your context. Parameter entities, which are used only in the DTD, use a different syntax, both in declaration

```
<!ENTITY % myParameterEntity "Class">
```

and in references to them:

%myParameterEntity;

Unparsed entities are referenced by names contained in attribute values declared to be of type ENTITY or ENTITIES.

Predefined Entities

XML processors recognize a number of entity references as referring to five characters that have special meaning when used in XML documents. This means that a character being used literally in content can be distinguished from its use as part of markup. The five entity references and the characters that they represent are listed here:

- amp—Represents the ampersand character (&) in parsed character data

- apos—Represents the apostrophe (') in parsed character data

- gt—Represents the right angle bracket (>) in parsed character data

- lt—Represents the left angle bracket (<) in parsed character data

- quot—Represents a single double quotation mark (") in parsed character data

Let's consider parsed entities and parameter entities in more detail.

Parsed Entities

In XML, an entity may contain parsed data or unparsed data. The term *parsed data* refers to data in XML syntax that is to be parsed—it doesn't mean that it has already been parsed. Similarly, the term *unparsed data* refers to data that is not intended to be parsed by an XML processor.

 Note Parsed entities are also *general entities* because they are used within the XML document rather than in the DTD. An internal parsed entity and an internal general entity are the same thing.

Parsed data consists of characters, which may represent either character data or markup.

```
<name>John Smith</name>
```

The preceding line of code consists of characters. The characters John Smith are character data, and the start tag <name> and the end tag </name> make up the markup.

You can represent the preceding code in an entity declaration for either an internal parsed entity or an external parsed entity. An internal parsed entity would have an entity declaration that declares a value:

```
<!ENTITY myNameInfo "<name>John Smith</name>" >
```

Notice that it is permissible to used tags with literal < and > characters within the quotation marks that contain the replacement text for the parsed entity.

An external parsed entity would provide an external reference using an appropriate combination of the SYSTEM and PUBLIC keywords. For example, if the replacement text for the entity was contained in a file myNameInfo.xml in the same directory as the document entity, you could declare the external parsed entity as follows:

```
<!ENTITY myNameInfo SYSTEM "myNameInfo.xml">
```

The external file would contain the replacement text:

```
<name>John Smith</name>
```

Internal Parsed Entities

Internal entities are defined in the same XML document (the same document entity) as they are used in.

For example, in a document about XML 1.0, you might have the following structure:

```
<?xml version="1.0" ?>
<!DOCTYPE document [
<!ENTITY xml1.0 "Extensible Markup Language 1.0">
]>
<document>
<description>
In February 1998 &xml1.0; was finalized by the World Wide Web
Consortium and released as a W3C Recommendation.
</description>
</document>
```

The following entity declaration associates the entity name xml1.0 with the text Extensible Markup Language 1.0 as the *replacement text*:

```
<!ENTITY xml1.0 "Extensible Markup Language 1.0">
```

 Note You may use the character sequence XML or xml to begin the name of an entity. You cannot use that character sequence to begin an element type name.

Then, in the content of the description element, the xml1.0 entity is referenced.

The XML processor processes the description element as if it reads as follows:

```
<description>
In February 1998 Extensible Markup Language 1.0 was finalized
by the World Wide Web Consortium and released as a W3C
Recommendation.
</description>
```

One example of entities' use in short documents is in SVG documents to define style information for several elements. For example, you could use an entity to define a red stroke on text and a rectangle shape:

```
<?xml version="1.0" ?>
<!DOCTYPE svg PUBLIC "-//W3C//DTD SVG 1.0//EN"
http://www.w3.org/Graphics/SVG/1.0/DTD/svg10.dtd[
<!ENTITY myRedStroke "fill:red">
]>
<svg>
<rect x="20" y="20" width="100" height="100"
 style="&myRedStroke" />
<text x="140" y="20" style="&myRedStroke">
This text is red
</text>
</svg>
```

Of course, typically, the style information in an SVG document is significantly longer to justify use of an entity in this way.

External Parsed Entities

External parsed entities are contained in a file external to the document entity.

The simplest situation is one in which an external parsed entity is referenced using an entity reference in the document entity, as shown earlier.

However, an external parsed entity may contain any arbitrary well-formed XML, including entity references. That means that an external parsed entity may itself contain an entity reference to yet another external parsed entity. Of course, in principle, that external parsed entity could contain yet further entity references to more external parsed entities.

It is in situations such as the one just described that an entity may indirectly refer back to itself. If that occurs, the XML document, taken as a whole, is not well formed. Remember that recursion is not allowed (refer back to Chapter 3, "XML Must Be Well-Formed"), so an error is signaled.

Text Declaration

An external parsed entity may optionally begin with a *text declaration*.

A full XML document can contain an XML declaration to indicate that the document is XML, to indicate the version of XML being used, and, optionally, to indicate whether the XML document is standalone and which character encoding is being used. In an external parsed entity, there is, by definition, no possibility that it is standalone. A text declaration, therefore, cannot have a `standalone` attribute.

A text declaration takes two forms. This first is this:

```
<?xml version="1.0" ?>
```

Here, the only attribute is the compulsory version attribute. An encoding attribute also is possible, as in this example:

```
<?xml version="1.0" encoding="UTF-8" ?>
```

Unparsed Entities

Unparsed entities are used in attribute values and are referenced by name. If the name of an unparsed entity appears in an attribute value declared as being of type `ENTITY` or `ENTITIES`, a validating XML processor must pass both the system identifier and the public identifier for the unparsed entity to the application.

The content of an unparsed entity may be text or other types of data. If it is text, then it can be XML or some other format.

An unparsed entity is declared using the following format:

```
<!ENTITY entityName SYSTEM "myPicture.gif" NDATA gif>
```

The *entityName* is used in attribute values to reference the unparsed entity. The filename of the entity is given in quotation marks following the SYSTEM keyword. The keyword NDATA indicates that the data is non-XML data. In this example, the unparsed entity is identified as being in GIF format, by means of a gif notation declared elsewhere in the DTD.

> **Note** A *notation* identifies by name the format of unparsed entities.

Declaring Notations

Notations are declared using the following general format:

```
<!NOTATION notationName locationOfInformation >
```

The *notationName* specifies the name of the notation. The *locationOfInformation* variable uses the SYSTEM and/or PUBLIC keywords to identify a resource where the application can access further information about the non-XML data indicated by the notation. This enables the application to further process the non-XML data, either using its own facilities or by accessing a helper application.

Types of Unparsed Data

Unparsed data might be an image, text, or binary data. The only responsibility of the XML processor is to pass to the application the name of the unparsed entity and the notation associated with it.

Parameter Entities

Parameter entities are used only in DTDs. They allow reuse of information within the DTD.

Suppose that you had a document of the following structure:

```
<Reports>
<Report>
<Introduction>
<!-- Introductory text goes here. -->
</Introduction>
<!-- Main report information goes here. -->
<Comment>
This contains a comment about an individual report
</Comment>
</Report>
</Reports>
```

If you were declaring a single introduction element, you might write the declaration as follows:

```
<!ELEMENT introduction (#PCDATA)>
```

Similarly, if you were declaring the comment element, you might write this:

```
<!ELEMENT comment (#PCDATA)>
```

The literal text (#PCDATA) is being used more than once, so you could use a parameter entity to replace it.

Remember that parameter entities are not permitted in the internal subset of a DTD; you need two separate documents.

The modified XML document would look like this:

```
<?xml version='1.0'?>
<!DOCTYPE Names SYSTEM "myDTD.dtd">
<Reports>
<Report>
<Introduction>
<!-- Introductory text goes here. -->
</Introduction>
<!-- Main report information goes here. -->
<Comment>
This contains comment about an individual report
</Comment>
</Report>
</Reports>
```

The external subset of the DTD could look like this:

```
<!ENTITY % myPC "(#PCDATA)" >
<!ELEMENT Reports (Report)+ >
<!ELEMENT Report (Introduction, Comment)>
<!ELEMENT Introduction %myPC; >
<!ELEMENT Comment %myPC; >
```

The literal text (#PCDATA) has been defined as the replacement text for the myPC parameter entity, declared as follows:

```
<!ENTITY % myPC "(#PCDATA)" >
```

You can then use the myPC parameter entity in the entity declarations for the Introduction and Comment elements:

```
<!ELEMENT Introduction %myPC; >
<!ELEMENT Comment %myPC; >
```

This example is very simple, but it indicates how a parameter entity can be used.

Summary

In this lesson, you learned what an entity is and what types of entities are defined for XML 1.0. You also learned how to declare parsed entities, unparsed entities, and parameter entities. In addition, you saw examples of how entities can be used.

LESSON 6
Characters in XML

In this lesson, you will learn about character sets and encodings and how they can be used with XML documents.

Internationalization

Only a few years ago, the World Wide Web was primarily an English-language medium, at least in the eyes of people from the United States and the United Kingdom. Of course, English is the native language of perhaps 10% of the world's population and is used in economically influential countries, with international trade, and particularly in countries where English is spoken natively. Support for English on the Web was obviously essential, but over several years it became increasingly obvious that support for many other languages was essential, too, if the Web is to be truly worldwide.

> **Note** In this lesson, you will learn many terms relating to characters that have very specific meanings. If you are unfamiliar with this material, you might find the new terminology a little confusing. It will make sense if you work through it slowly.

Support for multiple languages raises many issues for people who think primarily or exclusively in English. For example, how do you express characters that cannot simply be typed using an English-language keyboard? For example, how do you express characters in German that use

the umlaut, such as ü, or letters in French that have an acute accent above
a vowel, such as é?

> **Note**   The idea of internationalization is an impor-
> tant one in the XML world. Because *internationaliza-*
> *tion* is a long word, you will often see it abbreviated
> as i18n.

To understand how to solve this general problem, you need to consider
how characters are encoded.

Character Encodings

This section looks at how individual characters and sets of characters are
encoded on a computer.

As mentioned earlier, English characters can be entered into computer
memory most simply from the keyboard. However, at a fundamental level,
computers understand only numbers. A character must be represented in
some way as a number so that you can use text in a computer. A mapping
from a set of numbers to a set of characters is stored internally.

English-language characters (plus some other characters) can be represented using the American Standard Coding for Information Interchange
(ASCII) coding. This is an 8-bit coding system. All English characters can
be represented using the 256 characters (2^8) characters of ASCII. The
hexadecimal number 21, for example, corresponds to the exclamation
mark character (!).

> **Note**   The characters up to hexadecimal 0020 don't
> display a visible character onscreen, but they might
> affect screen appearance. Character 0020 (decimal 32),
> for example, is the space character.

Let's look at ASCII characters in a little more detail. If you are using a computer that is running a recent version of Microsoft Windows, you will have access to the Character Map, which allows you to express the ASCII character set as well as many non-English characters. You will use that to begin to explore some issues related to characters, their representation, and their display.

In Windows 2000, to access the Character Map, choose the Start button, Programs, System Tools, Character Map. When you run the Character Map utility, you will see the window shown in Figure 6.1.

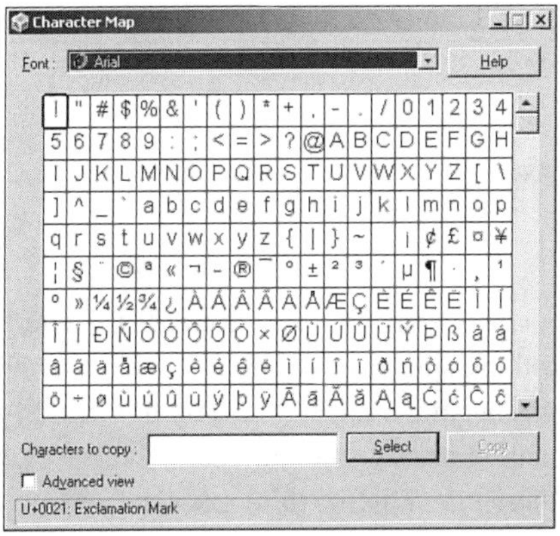

FIGURE 6.1 The Character Map utility in Windows 2000.

In this figure, the font applied initially is the Arial font. So, all characters displayed use the Arial font unless the user chooses an alternative font. We will return to the discussion of fonts a little later.

First, hover the mouse over the exclamation mark (!) in the top-left corner of the Character Map program. You will see a ToolTip:

```
U+0021 - Exclamation Mark
```

The meaning of the final part of the ToolTip is obvious: It is simply the natural English term for the character indicated by the mouse.

The U+0021 corresponds to the hexadecimal number 21, (decimal 33) mentioned earlier. However, it is an abbreviation indicating that the Unicode system (explained in greater detail later in the chapter) is in use and that the particular character is 0021. The 0021 is expressed in hexadecimal notation and would be expressed as 0033 in decimal notation.

Listing 6.1 shows an XML representation of the exclamation mark in hexadecimal and decimal notation, as well the literal exclamation mark character.

LISTING 6.1   Exclamations.xml: Expressing Characters in Hexadecimal and Decimal

```
<?xml version='1.0'?>
<exclamations>
<exc>&#x0021;</exc>
<exc>&#0033;</exc>
<exc>!</exc>
</exclamations>
```

If you run the code and display it in the Internet Explorer 5.5 browser, you will see something similar to Figure 6.2. Any other XML-compatible browser should give a similar appearance. Both *character references* display as an exclamation mark contained within the exc element, just like the literal exclamation mark in the third exc element.

Of course, what you have done so far you could have done more easily using an English-language keyboard. When you need to include characters that either are not available from an English language keyboard or can be achieved only using obscure key combinations, the Character Map utility becomes more helpful.

Suppose that you want to express the simple idea in German, "Übung macht den Meister" (meaning, "Practice makes perfect"). You need the *u* with the umlaut (also called a diaeresis). This can be copied from the Character Map by clicking the desired character and clicking the Copy button.

This enables you to include foreign-language characters that use the Roman alphabet in English-language documents. If you scroll down in the Character Map utility, you will see characters used in such languages as Russian, Hebrew, and Arabic.

```
 C:\My Writing\Sams - STY XML 10 Minutes\Ch06\Exclamations.xml - Microsoft Internet Explorer provided by AOL   _ 8 x

  File   Edit   View   Favorites   Tools   Help

  Back  ·  →  ·  ②  ③  ⚳   ③Search  ⚳Favorites  ⚳History   ⚳·  ⚳  ⚳  ⚳  ⚳

  Address  ⚳ C:\My Writing\Sams - STY XML 10 Minutes\Ch06\Exclamations.xml              ▼  ⚳Go   Links

       <?xml version="1.0" ?>
     - <exclamations>
          <exc>!</exc>
          <exc>!</exc>
          <exc>!</exc>
       </exclamations>




  ⚳ Done                                          ⚳ My Computer
```

FIGURE 6.2   Character references.

So, the type of facility supplied by the Character Map provides an answer sufficient for expressing many European and some Middle East languages. Of course, many languages cannot be expressed using the Character Map. For example, some Asian languages, such as Chinese, Japanese, and Korean, use many thousands of ideographic characters. An ideographic character represents a word or idea rather than an individual letter. A more general solution to supplying a desired character is needed to accommodate any written language.

XML and Internationalization

From the beginning, XML was intended to be used internationally. To support authentic international use, XML must be capable of expressing character sets used in all (or at least the most widely used) world languages. To achieve this international usage and express the ideas and words of many languages, XML has built on several other agreed approaches for expressing characters.

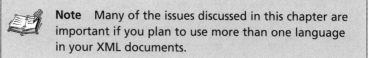

> **Note**   Many of the issues discussed in this chapter are important if you plan to use more than one language in your XML documents.

The 1-byte (8-bit) approach of the ASCII code is insufficient for expressing more than a few languages. Increasing the encoding to 2 bytes enables users to express far more characters (65,536 instead of 256).

Having 2-byte character codes opens up the possibility for many more codes than necessary to encode the characters of English and other languages that use the Roman alphabet. At the present time, the most widely used internationally accepted standard uses 16-bit encoding. It doesn't achieve representation of every single character that might be needed, but it does go further toward a truly global solution for character encoding.

All XML processors are required to support two particular character forms: UTF-8 and UTF-16. These are 8-bit and 16-bit forms of character encoding, respectively. In hexadecimal terms, these are numeric values from 0000 to FFFF inclusive, with minor gaps because some codes are used for other purposes.

The section "Unicode" looks a little more closely at these international codes. First, the next section looks again at how the encodings for individual characters can be expressed in a way that an XML processor will understand.

Character References

Character references are the XML technique for directly expressing the numeric character encoding of a character.

> **Note**   A *character reference* is a technique for using a numerical value, which can be expressed in hexadecimal or decimal notation, to refer to an individual character.

In XML, character references are used. To express a character reference using hexadecimal notation, use the character sequence &#x followed by four numeric characters or the characters A (decimal 10) to F (decimal 15) inclusive to express any character that can be expressed using 16-bit encoding. The end of the character reference is signaled by the semicolon (;).

Decimal numbers are expressed as &# followed by numbers up to 65,535 that are followed by a closing semicolon character.

An example using both hexadecimal and decimal notations is shown in Listing 6.2.

LISTING 6.2   Good.xml: A Statement in English and German

```
<?xml version='1.0'?>
<Good>
 <InEnglish>That is good.</InEnglish>
 <Deutsch>Das ist g&#x00FC;t.</Deutsch>
 <Deutsch>Das ist g&#252;t.</Deutsch>
</Good>
```

The desired character in German is represented numerically as hexadecimal 00FC.

If the code is displayed in the Internet Explorer browser, the desired character appears similar to Figure 6.3.

The character code 00FC is a 2-byte code.

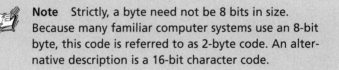

Note   Strictly, a byte need not be 8 bits in size. Because many familiar computer systems use an 8-bit byte, this code is referred to as 2-byte code. An alternative description is a 16-bit character code.

If you open the document shown in Listing 6.3 in your browser, you can explore the onscreen appearance of the full number of 16-bit characters by replacing the 16-bit number. Unfortunately, your computer probably will not have the necessary information to display many of the possible characters.

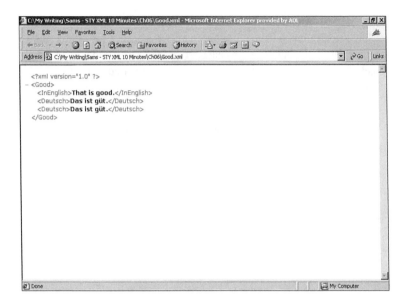

FIGURE 6.3   Displaying a foreign-language character using a character reference.

LISTING 6.3   Explore.xml: Explore the 16-Bit Character Encoding

```
<?xml version='1.0'?>
<Explore>
 <aCharacter>&#xFAFC;</aCharacter>
</Explore>
```

For many of the characters, you will find that a browser simply displays a square or other placeholder because your computer does not have a font to display the needed character.

Unicode

This section looks a little more closely at the character set that XML uses: Unicode.

> **Note**   Strictly speaking, XML uses the international Standard ISO/IEC 10646. Unfortunately, the International Organization for Standardization (ISO) does not make its standards freely available on the Web in the way that the World Wide Consortium (W3C) does. The Unicode encoding follows ISO/IEC 10646 and is accessible via the Web.

The Unicode organization created a character encoding that has global acceptance. Before the emergence of Unicode, many encoding schemes existed that, for many practical purposes, were incompatible. There is, of course, no intrinsic reason why a particular character—the exclamation mark, for example—should be represented by a particular number. Therefore, the encoding is arbitrary, to a degree. The important thing is that everybody agrees to use the same encoding.

Of course, it made sense for the English encoding to be compatible with the long-standing (in computer terms) ASCII encoding. So, English is expressed in Unicode codes beginning with a double zero, such as representing the exclamation mark with hexadecimal 0021.

> **Note**   Unicode is also used by many modern programming languages, including Java and ECMAScript (JavaScript). An understanding of at least the basics of Unicode is useful for the Web developer.

Unicode uses an initially intimidating technical vocabulary. See http://www.unicode.org/glossary/ for further details.

Unicode Supplementary Code Points

The latest versions of Unicode go beyond the hexadecimal range of 0000 to FFFF. Also included are *supplementary code points* in the range 100000 to 10FFFF. This provides for the encoding of additional characters that cannot be encoded in the 16-bit encoding.

Thus extended, Unicode allows the encoding of more than one million characters, which is anticipated to accommodate all of the world's characters. Of course, most of the most commonly used characters are included in the 16-bit encoding scheme.

The first 65,000 or so characters are referred to as the Basic Multilingual Plane—BMP, for short.

Unicode Encoding Forms

Unicode provides three *encoding forms*.

- UTF-8—An 8-bit encoding form. This must be supported by all XML processors. UTF-8 maps one to one with ASCII.

- UTF-16—A 16-bit encoding form. This must be supported by all conforming XML processors.

- UTF-32—A 32-bit encoding form. XML 1.0 processors are not obligated to support this encoding form.

Fonts, Characters, and Glyphs

This section examines the meaning of the terms *font*, *character*, and *glyph*.

A Unicode character point is a numerical representation of a conceptual character. For example, suppose that you refer to "uppercase *A*." If you are familiar with English, you know which character is being referred to. However, you can't say with certainty exactly how this conceptual character will be displayed onscreen or on paper. This is where glyphs and fonts come in.

For the purposes of this discussion, a *font* is a set of glyphs. A *glyph* is a particular visual representation of a character. Any character, such as the uppercase *A*, can be displayed in any number of visual appearances.

This truth is illustrated using Scalable Vector Graphics (SVG). Listing 6.4 shows a simple SVG document with elements that contain the uppercase character sequence XML, displayed in several different fonts. To run and view the code, you will need an SVG viewer, such as the Adobe SVG Viewer (www.adobe.com/svg/).

LISTING 6.4   myXML.svg: Displaying the Same Characters As Different Glyphs Specified by Different Fonts

```
<?xml version='1.0'?>
<svg>
<text x="20" y="30" style="font-size:30; font-
family:Arial; ">XML</text>
<text x="20" y="70" style="font-size:30; font-family:Arial; ">
&#x0058;&#x004D;&#x004C;</text>
<text x="20" y="110" style="font-size:30; font-family:'Times
New Roman';">
XML</text>
<text x="20" y="150" style="font-size:30; font-family:'Times
New Roman';">&#x0058;&#x004D;&#x004C;</text>
</svg>
```

Notice the difference between the second and third lines of characters. The glyphs that are displayed in the second line form part of the Arial font. Glyphs in the Arial font share visual features in common. An important one is that they all lack a *serif*, those little marks at the ends of strokes on some characters. The same characters, XML, are represented by different glyphs when the Times New Roman font is used, as in the third line in Figure 6.4. The glyphs in that font commonly possess a serif on many letters. Compare the exact shape of the characters XML as displayed in Figure 6.4 to see the differences.

Whether the XML is specified as literal characters or as character references, the displayed characters are the same if the font is the same. You can see this in the first two myXML elements shown in Figure 6.4.

The range of glyphs available for English-language characters is enormous, in part expressing the creativity of font designers. For XML application languages, the character point is conceptually the same regardless of the visual appearance chosen to display it.

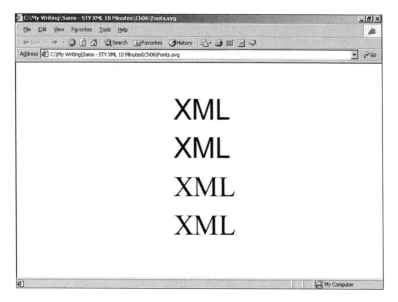

FIGURE 6.4   Literal characters or character references yield the same result.

Summary

In this lesson, you learned about the need for internationalization and how XML supports it. Several technical terms, including *character*, *font*, and *glyph*, were introduced and explained. The concepts of character encoding, character set, Unicode, and character references also were discussed, along with examples.

LESSON 7

The Logic Hidden in XML

In this chapter, you will learn how data can be modeled using XML and how the W3C models of logical structure behind well-formed or valid XML can be represented and manipulated.

Modeling Data As XML

Earlier chapters in this book described XML mostly in terms of a set of syntax rules that define how sequences of characters are to be used so that an XML processor can process an XML document without throwing errors and that also define the physical structure, expressed as entities. But XML documents also have a logical structure that is expressed by the nesting of elements and the presence of attributes on selected elements. This highly flexible document structure means that you can model many types of data. This is useful for modeling both highly regular structured data that might otherwise be stored in a relational database and highly flexible narrative documents.

First, let's look at issues relating to markup languages and see why they are increasingly used in place of or alongside binary file formats.

Binary Files and Markup

Binary files play an important role in data storage because they are—or can be—very compact for any given amount of data to be stored. When RAM was measured in kilobytes rather than hundreds of megabytes and when disk storage was measured in megabytes rather than tens of giga-bytes, compactness of storage was crucially important to developers of software for personal computers. As quantities of RAM and hard disk storage have multiplied in recent years, compactness of data has become less important for many uses. The increase in the availability of RAM and hard disk space has outpaced the availability of developer time to create programs to handle data.

Many more types of data are being stored than were in use a decade or so ago. Typically binary files are specific to a particular application or vendor; programs to make them comprehensible to humans with onscreen displays or paper reports are becoming progressively more complex.

Thus, new types of data storage must be easy to create and maintain, not just be compact. Markup languages in general, and XML in particular, play a part in the process of making data easier to structure and describe. Clear data structures that can be easily modified or adapted, together with processors that access the data contained in those structures, make it easier to create, maintain, and modify data storage than when using binary files alone.

One of the best known attempts to use markup languages to store or display structured data is the Hypertext Markup Language (HTML).

XML More Structured Than HTML

HTML was initially designed to provide structured documents. HTML has enjoyed enormous success as the language used by Web browsers to display information, but it has fundamental limitations with structuring data. Look at the short employment record expressed in the HTML code in Listing 7.1.

LISTING 7.1   An HTML Representation of Structured Data

```
<html>
<body>
<h1>Peter Jones</h1>
<h2>Basic data</h2>
<p>1958/10/29</p>
<p>ABC123</p>
<h2>Employee History</h2>
<p>Peter Jones was first employed by the company on January
   21st 1980.
```

LISTING 7.1   Continued

```
He has performed well since then and has been promoted four
times.</p>
</body>
</html>
```

An h1 element is used to provide a heading for the employee data that follows. The h1 element has a hybrid function: It communicates something about how its content will be displayed and also indicates something (rather vaguely) about the nature of the content in the overall structure of the document. An h1 element indicates a heading, but an h1 element in one HTML document might have a different importance or meaning than an h1 element in another HTML document in the same subject domain.

The fact that an h1 element indicates a header is useful up to a point, but you learn nothing about what an h1 header *means*. Nor does the h1 element—or other HTML header elements—actually contain all the data related to that heading. For example, the h2 element in this example does not actually contain the p element that describes Peter Jones's employment history. The content of the h2 element and the following p element are logically related but are structurally only loosely related.

If the HTML document contained four employee records, you have to depend on the good sense of the Web page author for any consistency in structure. You might use an h1 element to indicate that multiple records are involved but that the h1 element is only a descriptor, not a container element.

Taken together, these characteristics of HTML mean that it can structure data, but this structure is loosely expressed and is mixed with presentation data. For simple data, that might be acceptable. However, as the complexity of data and its volume increases—and as the prospect of more automatic processing of data appears on the horizon—the fuzzy edges of the structure that HTML provides become substantive disadvantages.

XML provides a cleaner, more consistent framework for expressing structured data. In part, this improvement relies on the fact that you can create meaningful element type names for each element in an XML document. In addition, by appropriately nesting XML elements, you can express more clearly the logical relationships among elements.

An XML document broadly equivalent to Listing 7.1 might look something like Listing 7.2.

LISTING 7.2   An XML Representation of Employee Data

```
<employee>
<name>Peter Jones</name>
<dateOfBirth>1958/10/29</dateOfBirth>
<employeeID>ABC123</employeeID>
<employeeHistory>
Peter Jones was first employed by the company on January 21st
1980. He has performed well since then and has been promoted
four times.
</employeeHistory>
</employee>
```

An enormous advantage of the XML approach is that there is a container element—in this case, the `employee` element—that contains all the data in an XML document. Everything nested within the `employee` element is logically related to that `employee` element. This is a structure that more closely approximates reality.

Assuming that the element type name of the document element in an XML document is chosen wisely, this also hints at what the data is about. For example, when you see an `employees` element, you can guess that the content likely relates to data about a group of employees. An `h1` element type name can't communicate that—at least, not in the element name.

When element type names are chosen sensibly, XML can be termed self-describing data. An `employee` element tells much more about the data contained in it than, for example, an `html` or `body` element in an HTML document. In addition to creating new element type names, you can create new attributes to express information about individual elements for particular purposes.

Similarly, each component part of the `employee` element—whether attributes or children or descendant elements—can be viewed as further describing the `employee` element. In this respect, the content of an XML element has similarities to the properties of a programming object. Just as encapsulation is useful in programming languages, nesting of elements is useful for data description.

Let's move on to look at how you can use XML to describe various broad types of data.

Modeling Relational-Type Data

XML allows the modeling of data that would conventionally be stored in a relational database-management system.

> **Note** In some systems, data is served as XML but is stored in a relational database-management system (RDBMS) because of the highly optimized storage provided.

Relational data is typically expressed as rows (records) and columns (fields). A simple RDBMS table might contain employee records. Each record might consist of an employee's ID number, surname, first name, initials, and date of birth. This can be easily modeled in XML. Listing 7.3 shows one approach.

LISTING 7.3 Modeling an Employee Record in XML

```
<?xml version='1.0'?>
<employees>
<employee>
 <employeeID>ABC123</employeeID>
 <surname>Cameron</surname>
 <firstName>Ewen</firstName>
 <initials></initials>
 <dateOfBirth>1975/12/28</dateOfBirth>
</employee>
<!-- Other "records" can go here -->
</employees>
```

XML provides flexibility in how the logical relationships are expressed. For example, you can use attributes to express information that might be contained in a child element. For example, you could use an attribute to express the employee ID, as in Listing 7.4.

LISTING 7.4 An Alternate Structure for Representing the Data of Listing 7.3

```
<?xml version='1.0'?>
<employees>
<employee employeeID='ABC123'>
  <surname>Cameron</surname>
  <firstName>Ewen</firstName>
  <initials></initials>
  <dateOfBirth>1975/12/28</dateOfBirth>
</employee>
<!-- Other "records" can go here -->
</employees>
```

Thus, the same information has multiple possible representations in XML. The flexibility of XML creates potential problems because one logical structure can be expressed in more than one way. As you will see in Chapter 11, "XSLT—Transforming XML Structure," you can use the Extensible Stylesheet Language Transformations (XSLT) to transform XML data from one equivalent structure to another (as well as perform other transformation tasks described in Chapter 10, "XSLT—Creating HTML from XML," and Chapter 12, "XSLT—Sorting XML").

In the approach shown in Listing 7.3 and Listing 7.4, the XML document corresponds broadly to an Employees table in an RDBMS system. Each employee element holds a record, in RDBMS terms. Each column is represented by an XML element, such as the employeeID element.

You can even express a single row as follows:

```
<employee
employeeID="ABC123"
surname="Cameron"
firstName="Ewen"
initials=""
dateOfBirth="1975/12/28"
>
```

Using only attributes confines you to the equivalent of a row structure of an RDBMS approach.

When the data naturally follows a relational structure, ultimate storage may best be in a proprietary format.

Hierarchical Data in XML

Some types of data do not follow the regular structure of rows and columns that occur in RDBMS tables. For example, you could express a date store for the support calls from a customer as follows:

```
<customer customerID="DCE789">
 <call date="2002/08/30">
  <subject>Program crashes when started</subject>
  <supportOperator>Jim<supportOperator>
  <status>Resolved</status>
 </call>
 <call date="2002/09/25">
  <subject>Was unable to locate command to print.</subject>
  <supportOperator>Karen<supportOperator>
  <status>Resolved</status>
 </call>
</customer>
```

This support record for a single customer has a hierarchy—each customer element has nested inside it one or more call elements. In turn, each call element has three child elements—subject element, support element, and status element.

In data structures that model hierarchical relationships, XML can cope with hierarchies of arbitrary complexity. As hierarchies in data increase in depth, it becomes increasingly problematic for an RDBMS to model the data.

Loosely Structured Data in XML

XML is derived from the Standard Generalized Markup Language (SGML). SGML often is used for complex documents, such as aircraft maintenance manuals. Because SGML is useful for expressing complex documents, it is not surprising that XML is also used to express documents of significant complexity.

> **Note** All XML files are usually referred to as "docu-
> ments." XML documents are often referred to as
> document-centric and data-centric. The former describes
> simple letters or other correspondence, as well as
> lengthy documents that would take up multiple vol-
> umes if printed out. Data-centric XML "documents"
> use XML to store data that conventionally would be
> stored, for example, in an RDBMS or a hierarchical
> database.

Some lengthy document-centric XML documents are very rigidly structured, although they are documents rather than "data." On the other hand,
XML can be used to contain documents that form a very loose or flexible
structure that might build on this sort of form:

```
<book>
<introduction>
<!-- Text for the introduction goes here, perhaps in multiple
 <section> or <paragraph> elements -- >
</introduction>
<chapter number="1">
<!-- In more highly structured documents, we may also have
 <section> elements -- >
<paragraph>Some paragraph text</paragraph>
<paragraph>Some more paragraph text</paragraph>
</chapter>
<!-- An appendix or several might go here. -->
<!-- An index, with many variant structures might be added
 here. -->
</book>
```

The structure shown is simple and clear, but many real-life uses are much
more complex. In some cases, you might add elements such as header,
subheading, footnote, sidebar, and other possible elements that convey
the great diversity of structures used in books. XML can express all these
structures.

As you have seen, XML can express the logical relationships contained in
relational-type data, hierarchical data, and loosely structured data. For certain uses, non-XML approaches might be more efficient or appropriate,

but the sheer flexibility of XML makes it an important technology to master if you are handling anything but small amounts of data.

The final sections of this chapter briefly look at how XML data can be accessed and manipulated programmatically. Some of the topics introduced, including the Document Object Model and XPath, are discussed later in the book.

W3C XML Data Models

XML documents follow the syntax rules of well-formedness but also represent *data objects* that have a hierarchical structure. The hierarchical structure must exist for each XML document, given that there is a document entity within which the prolog (if it exists), the document element, and all other elements exist. The simplest hierarchy for a well-formed XML document is a document entity with a single document element contained inside it.

The World Wide Web Consortium has produced three families of specifications that express, in different ways, the logical structure of an XML document: the Document Object Model, the XML Path Language, and the XML Information Set.

The Document Object Model

The Document Object Model (DOM) for XML documents is, at its simplest, closely related to the DOM for HTML documents. The W3C has created specifications that express increasing functionality as subsequent *levels* of the DOM. The development of the DOM is ongoing—Level 1 and Level 2 have been released as full W3C specifications. DOM Level 3 is under development at the time of this writing.

As its name suggests, the DOM *models* an XML *document* in terms of *objects*. Technically, the DOM specifications govern *interfaces*. Interfaces can be viewed as contracts with an object. It doesn't matter what the exact structure of an object is. However, if it is a DOM object, it must behave as if particular properties and methods exist for the object.

The DOM enables developers to manipulate the in-memory representation of an XML document, with each element and attribute represented as a node in the in-memory hierarchy. The fundamental interface in the DOM is the Node interface. The nodes for elements, attributes, and so on extend the Node interface. You can add nodes that represent elements, attributes, and so on. The in-memory representation can be discarded after the application has performed any necessary actions; it also can be explicitly saved to a new file or can alter the file that was loaded.

The Document Object Model is discussed in more detail in Chapter 16, "The Document Object Model," and Chapter 17, "The Document Object Model, 2."

XPath

The XML Path Language (XPath) also models an XML document as a set of nodes. However, the hierarchy of nodes in the XPath representation of an XML document differs in several respects from the DOM representation.

XPath uses a path syntax to express the hierarchy of the content in an XML document. XPath bears similarities to the *paths*—hence the name XML Path Language—used to express the hierarchy of the file system on your computer.

The *root node* of an XPath document, which is equivalent to the document entity, is expressed as a single forward slash character (/). Nodes can then be accessed relative to the root node. For example, the document element of a document with a document element called myDocumentElement can be accessed using path syntax, /myDocumentElement.

XPath is intended for use with other XML specifications, such as XSLT and XForms (a new forms language expressed in XML). XPath specifies which part of an XML document is to be processed. For example, XPath can be used with XSLT to select a set of nodes that, not surprisingly, it terms a *node-set*. The node-set is then processed in one of the ways supported by the XSLT specification.

XPath is discussed in greater detail in Chapter 9, "The XML Path Language—XPath."

The XML Information Set

The XML Information set, also termed the infoset, is an abstract data model for most of an XML document and is intended to be used by other XML-related specifications from the W3C.

An information item is similar to a node as used by DOM and XPath. However, the detail of how an XML document is modeled differs from both DOM and XPath.

The XML information set is the newest of the data models specified by the W3C but is viewed as the foundation for many future XML-related specifications produced by the W3C. For example, the infoset is used as a basis for the W3C XML Schema language, together with some augmentation of that infoset to express notions specific to the activity of schema validation.

Which Data Model?

The fact that the W3C has released three data models that model the same thing—an XML document—can seem confusing. In practice, the choice of data model to use depends on what you want to do.

The DOM is used when you want to create, manipulate, or delete parts of an XML document using programming languages such as Java. XPath is used primarily to navigate the in-memory representation of an XML document, to make selected parts of that document available to other XML-based application languages such as XSLT, the XML Pointer Language, and XForms.

The information set is used in W3C XML Schema and is proposed as the basis for the XML Query Language (XQuery) and version 2.0 of XSLT and XPath (currently under active development at the W3C).

Summary

XML can express, or model, many types of data structures, including structures that are similar to relational data, hierarchical data, and loosely structured data.

Data models provide the way for programming languages to efficiently and conveniently create, modify, or manipulate XML data. Three data models were introduced in this chapter—the Document Object Model, the XML Path Language, and the XML Information Set.

LESSON 8
Namespaces in XML

In this lesson, you will learn the reasons for using namespaces in XML documents and the correct syntax for XML namespaces.

What Is a Namespace, and Why Do You Need Them?

XML is useful for exchange of documents. A finite number of element type names is available to use to contain the document content. In a global Web, how do we handle the possibility of two element type names being the same? The solution that the W3C chose is namespaces.

 Note A *namespace* is a collection of names. In XML, a namespace refers to a collection of element type names and attribute names.

So, exactly why do we need namespaces? You might have document fragments such as the following:

```
<html>
<head>
<title>My XHTML document</title>
</head>
<body>Some content.</body>
</html>
```

and

```
<persons>
<person>
<title>President</title>
<firstName>George</firstName>
<lastName>Bush</lastName>
</person>
</persons>
```

Even with simple documents that mix these two XML structures, there is
a problem. In this example, how do you distinguish unambiguously the
`title` element that belongs to XHTML from the `title` element in the
`persons` data store? When you mix longer documents, possibly using
more than two vocabularies, the potential for problems is greater.

Three important problems almost inevitably might arise:

- It is difficult to recognize the application to be used for processing particular elements.

- Elements with the same element type name are used for different
  real-world meanings.

- Different element type names are used by different users or
  groups of users to represent the same real-world notion.

XML namespaces were designed to overcome the first two problems. A
solution to the third problem using XSLT is described in Chapter 11,
"XSLT—Transforming XML Structure."

Recognizing Which Application to Use

In the preceding code, how do you signal that a Web browser should process the `title` element from the XHTML code snippet and that another application should process the `title` element from the `persons` data store?

The first code snippet could be nested within the second, or vice versa. So, you need a mechanism that solves the problem, regardless of which essentially infinite number of structures is used. You need to be able to identify the individual elements as belonging to a particular namespace.

Element Type Name Clashes

Element type names clash when two or more XML document authors use the same element type name to represent different real-world ideas or values.

Because the community using XML is already large and will grow further, the possibility that element type names will clash in shared documents becomes very real. The likelihood of element name clashes also increases as more XML documents are shared outside defined groups.

Consider the possibility of sharing information from several sources, each of which uses an `order` element:

```
<order>
 <orderNumber>AB123</orderNumber>
 <Items>
  <Item number="20">Ink cartridges</Item>
  <Item number="2">3.5" Floppy Disks (Box of 10)</Item>
 </Items>
</order>
```

The `order` element has a different meaning in the following code:

```
<order>
 <givenBy>General B. Smart</givenBy>
 <Content>Relocate 6 jet fighters to MacDill Air Force
   Base</Content>
</order>
```

It is different again in the following code:

```
<order>
 <Location>Seattle</Location>
 <Description>A riot lasted several hours following clashes
 with anti-globalization protesters.
</order>
```

> **Note** These examples illustrate the problem, but more subtle issues also arise. Suppose that several companies each use an order element to refer to the placing of an order for goods and services. Those companies are not obligated to use an order element with the same structure of child and descendant elements nested within it.

If these XML documents remained within commercial, military, or police organizations, possibly no confusion would arise. However, suppose that the police or the Air Force ordered a number of items from the supplier that uses the order element in the first of the three ways shown. How is the reader—and, more importantly, an XML processor—to know which order element is intended in any particular context?

Clearly, a mechanism is needed to distinguish a commercial order from a military order or an order recorded by a police department. You need to be able to express in XML similar distinctions.

In XML, elements are distinguished by using *namespaces*.

> **Note** A namespace is simply a collection of names. In XML 1.0, a namespace doesn't imply any particular document structure. It simply expresses the notion that these elements belong together.

A concept similar to XML namespaces exists in some programming languages. For example, in Java, a particular class must have a unique name, to avoid ambiguity. In Java, a *package* provides a broad equivalent to the concept of XML namespaces. A class must have a name that is unique within a package. Classes in other packages might have the same class name, but because they are in a different package, there is no risk of confusion as the code is processed.

As in Java, each XML element in an XML namespace must have a unique name; otherwise, confusion can arise.

Let's move on to examine exactly how XML distinguishes namespaces.

Using Namespaces in XML

To clearly distinguish the order element here you would need to provide more information about the element type name than simply order:

```
<order>
 <givenBy>General B. Smart</givenBy>
 <Content>Relocate 6 jet fighters to MacDill Air Force
  Base</Content>
</order>
```

from the order element here

```
<order>
 <Location>Seattle</Location>
 <Description>A riot lasted several hours following clashes
  with anti-globalization protesters.
</order>
```

The solution to this, in XML 1.0, is a *qualified name*. This is often abbreviated as QName.

 A *qualified name* is an XML element type name that consists of two parts—a *namespace prefix* and a *local part* separated by the colon character (:).

Qualified Names

You can distinguish elements using qualified names (QNames). Referring back to the earlier example, the military version of an order could use the QName mil:order. This would distinguish it from possible QNames for the other two order element types, perhaps expressed as business:order and civil:order.

Each QName consists of a namespace prefix, a colon character, and a local part. The local part is what we have called the element type name in a non–namespace-aware document.

 Note   The colon character can legally be used for any purpose in XML. To avoid confusion and unpredictable results, it is wise to reserve the use of the colon character as a separator in QNames only.

If you use QNames on their own, you might run into problems similar to those you are trying to avoid. For example, the mil:order element might itself lead to ambiguity. Are you referring to military orders or militia orders? Similarly, if you refer to business:order elements, which of potentially many element types created by individual businesses or consortia are you referring to?

You need a more universal way to distinguish namespaces than simply using namespace prefixes alone. You achieve potentially unique identification of a namespace using a uniform resource identifier and mapping a namespace prefix to it.

URIs Represent Namespaces

In XML namespaces, the *namespace name* is a uniform resource identifier (URI).

A URI is a potentially lengthy sequence of characters. For example, you might want to create a document type for a particular structure of document. You could choose a namespace URI `http://www.XMML.com/myVeryOwnNamespace`.

So, why aren't URIs used directly in QNames? Three reasons are worth mentioning:

First, URIs often make use of the colon character as a separator. With the following start tag, ambiguity exists regarding which of the two colon characters is the separator between the namespace prefix and the local part:

```
<http://www.XMML.com/myVeryOwnNamespace:document>
```

Does this refer to an element whose namespace prefix is `http` and local part is `//www.XMML.com/myVeryOwnNamespace:document`, or does this refer to an element whose namespace prefix is `http://www.XMML.com/myVeryOwnNamespace` and local part is `document`? For the human reader, it is pretty obvious that the second possibility is much more likely; for an XML processor, however, serious ambiguity arises.

Second, if you write elements using the literal URI throughout the XML document, it would soon become difficult for a human reader to decipher what the document is about. This is particularly true if lines must be broken to squeeze the lengthy URI onto the page:

```
<http://www.XMML.com/myVeryOwnNamespace:document>
 <http://www.XMML.com/myVeryOwnNamespace:introduction>
  Some content goes here.
 </http://www.XMML.com/myVeryOwnNamespace:introduction>
<!-- Many more lengthy elements could go here. -->
</http://www.XMML.com/myVeryOwnNamespace:document>
```

Third, URIs can contain characters that are not allowed in XML names.

The problem is solved by using a succinct namespace prefix that complies with the rules for XML names and that is mapped to a namespace URI. Declaring a namespace involves associating the namespace prefix with the namespace URI. In XML, you do this using a special type of attribute called a *namespace declaration*.

Namespace Declarations

To be used in an XML document, a namespace must be declared. A namespace declaration is made in the start tag of the element to which it refers.

A namespace declaration has a special structure. For most namespace declarations, the attribute name begins with the character sequence xmlns, followed by a colon and the namespace prefix. These are followed by an equal sign (=) and the namespace URI enclosed in a pair of double or single quotation marks:

```
xmlns:namespacePrefix='namespaceURI'
```

> **Note** XML names that begin with the character sequence XML (in any case combination) are reserved for W3C use, as in the namespace declarations demonstrated in this section. As a result, do not attempt to create your own namespace named xml:.

The document element in the http://www.XMML.com/myVeryOwnNamespace namespace can be declared as follows, assuming that you map the namespace URI to the namespace prefix XMML:

```
<XMML:document xmlns:XMML="http://www.XMML.com/
myVeryOwnNamespace>
```

The short sample document then would be written as follows:

```
<XMML:document
 xmlns:XMML="http://www.XMML.com/myVeryOwnNamespace>
  <XMML:introduction>
    Some content goes here.
  </XMML:introduction>
  <!-- Many more lengthy elements could go here. -->
</XMML:document>
```

The alternative form of namespace declaration is the character sequence xmlns followed by the equal sign and the namespace URI enclosed in paired quotation marks:

```
xmlns="namespaceURI"
```

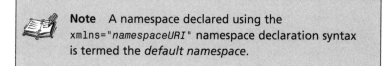

Note A namespace declared using the
xmlns="*namespaceURI*" namespace declaration syntax
is termed the *default namespace*.

Using this approach, you could express your document as follows:

```
<document
   xmlns="http://www.XMML.com/myVeryOwnNamespace>
   <introduction>
   Some content goes here.
   </introduction>
 <!-- Many more lengthy elements could go here. -->
</document>
```

For the human reader, the immediately preceding version is perhaps easier
to read, but the earlier version using the XMML namespace prefix is less
ambiguous. For the XMML processor, these documents are identical in a
namespace sense. All the elements in each document are associated with
the namespace URI http://www.XMML.com/myVeryOwnNamespace, and the
XML processor uses the namespace URI for identifying namespaces.

Caution Namespace URIs in XML must be identical
before they are considered to refer to the same namespace. So, if you create your own namespace, be sure
that you are totally consistent in how you use uppercase and lowercase characters.

If document authors use URIs for domains that they own or otherwise
legitimately use, a namespace URI should be unique. In addition, it is
important that namespace URIs are persistent, to instill confidence that
URIs and their related XML vocabularies remain stable.

> **Note**   The namespace URI need not point to any particular document. In particular, it need not contain any schema for the class of documents. The primary purpose of the namespace URI is to provide a unique and persistent identifier for an XML vocabulary.

Namespace declarations should be explicit in the start tag of an appropriate element or should be declared in the internal subset of the DTD. Namespace-aware processors are not required to be validating processors. Therefore, external declarations may not be accessed by a nonvalidating processor.

Namespaces and Attributes

An attribute is assumed to be in the same namespace as the element with which it is associated. The namespace prefix of the element need not be expressed on the attribute, too. For example, both the XMML:chapter element and the number attribute in the following code are in the same namespace:

```
<XMML:chapter
xmlns:XMML=http://www.XMML.com/ABookNamespace
number="3">
<!-- Chapter content goes here. -->
</XMML:chapter>
```

An attribute need not share the same namespace prefix as the start tag on which it is placed. You have seen this already for the reserved attributes whose qualified names begin with the character sequence xmlns.

More generally, to use an attribute with a different namespace, the namespace prefix must be declared on either the element or an ancestor of it. Consider this example:

```
<someNamespace:someElement
xmlns:someNamespace=http://www.XMML.com/someNamespace
xmlns:someOtherNamespace=http://www.XMML.com/someOtherNamespace
someOtherNamespace:someAttribute="something"
/>
```

In principle, the value of an XML attribute may contain the colon character. However, in namespace-aware XML documents, if the attribute is declared to be of type ID, IDREF, IDREFS, ENTITY, ENTITIES, or NOTATION, use of the colon character is not permitted.

Namespace Well-Formedness

The "Namespaces in XML" Recommendation (http://www.w3.org/TR/1999/REC-xml-names-19990114), or, more precisely, an erratum to it (http://www.w3.org/XML/xml-names-19990114-errata), specifies a concept of namespace well-formedness.

Namespace well-formedness includes the XML well-formedness criteria defined in Chapter 2, "The Structure of an XML Document," and Chapter 3, "XML Must Be Well-Formed," together with the following constraints:

- Element type names and attribute names may contain either zero or one colon characters.

- No entity names or processing instruction targets or notation names may contain a colon character.

- No attribute that is declared to be of type ID, IDREF, ENTITY, ENTITIES, or NOTATION may contain a colon character in its value.

Using Multiple Namespaces in a Document

Namespaces remove ambiguity from element type names. This assists the exchange of XML documents between users, but it also allows elements from different namespaces—in context implicitly different XML application languages—to be mixed in the same document.

You can mix elements in the same document if you understand the scope of namespaces.

Scope of Namespaces

The scope of a namespace is limited to all elements nested inside the element on which the namespace was declared. However, the namespace may be altered by a namespace declaration on any of the nested elements.

Look at a simple example:

```
<somePrefix:anElement xmlns:somePrefix=
  http://www.XMML.com/someNamespace>
  <anotherPrefix:anElement
  xmlns:anotherPrefix="http://www.XMML.com/anotherNamespace>
  Some content
  </anotherPrefix:anElement>
</somePrefix:anElement>
```

The `somePrefix:anElement` element has an `anotherPrefix:anElement` element nested inside it. The `somePrefix:anElement` element is associated with the namespace URI `http://www.XMML.com/someNamespace`. The namespace declaration on the `anotherPrefix:anElement` element associates the `anotherPrefix` namespace prefix with a different namespace URI: `http://www.XMML.com/anotherNamespace`.

Let's return to the earlier example and explore how `order` elements from different namespaces might be used in a single XML document.

You might have a document with a structure similar to the following from a police department to a supplier:

```
<PurchaseOrder
xmlns="http://MyWonderfulLocalPoliceDepartment.com/
  purchaseOrders">
<Reason>
<order>
 <Location>Seattle</Location>
 <Description>A riot lasted several hours following clashes
   with anti-globalization protesters.
</order>
</Reason>
<Supplier>
<business:order
   xmlns:business="http://SomeFriendlyLocalBusiness.com/
   PurchaseOrders">
```

```
<business:orderNumber>
 AB123
</business:orderNumber>
<business:Items>
 <business:Item number="20">Tear Gas Cartridges
  </business:Item>
 <business:Item number="10">Personal Protection Masks
   </business:Item>
 </business:Items>
</business:order>
</Supplier>
<PurchaseOrder>
```

Two namespace declarations exist. The first associates the default namespace with the namespace URI `http://MyWonderfulLocalPoliceDepartment.com/purchaseOrders`. The second, on the `business:order` element, associates the `business` namespace prefix with the namespace URI `http://SomeFriendlyLocalBusiness.com/PurchaseOrders`. You can clearly distinguish the `order` element in the default namespace from the `business:order` element. The XML processor uses the namespace URIs rather than the namespace prefixes to distinguish the namespaces.

Summary

The need for XML namespaces to accommodate the likelihood of element type name clashes was explained in this chapter.

XML 1.0 uses a namespace URI to uniquely identify a namespace. A namespace URI is mapped to a namespace prefix by means of a name-space declaration. A namespace-aware element type name consists of a *namespace prefix* and a *local part*.

LESSON 9

The XML Path Language— XPath

In this lesson, you will learn about the XML Path Language (XPath) and its view of an XML document. You also will learn how to use XPath to access nodes representing elements and attributes of XML documents.

How XPath Is Used

XPath is written in a non-XML syntax that enables you to define which part or parts of an XML document are selected by an XML processor or an application built on it. For example, you might want to select information to include in a company report from elements in a data store representing sales during a specified period.

Understanding basic XPath syntax is essential to being able to use Extensible Stylesheet Language Transformations (XSLT), described in Chapter 10, "XSLT—Creating HTML from XML"; Chapter 11, "XSLT— Transforming XML Structure"; and Chapter 12, "XSLT—Sorting XML."

> **Note** The description of XPath in this chapter focuses mostly on the selection of elements and attributes using the abbreviated XPath syntax. XPath also has an unabbreviated syntax.

To understand how to use XPath, you need to see how XPath models an XML document and how XPath syntax is used.

An XML Document As a Hierarchy of Nodes

The description of XML documents in earlier chapters focused mostly on the syntax of the document. However, in XPath, an XML document is treated as a logical structure and is viewed as a hierarchy of nodes.

Each XML document has an in-memory hierarchy that represents the logical structure of the document, not its surface syntax. The document entity is represented in XPath as the *root node*. The representation of any XML document has exactly one root node. Because all other parts of an XML document are logically related to the document entity, the root node that represents the document entity is the apex of the hierarchy of nodes.

For an XML document, as distinct from an external parsed entity, each root node must have exactly one *element node* child.

For a very simple XML document such as the following, the XPath structure is similar to that shown in Figure 9.1:

```
<?xml version="1.0" ?>
<document>
George Bush is the son of George Bush.
</document>
```

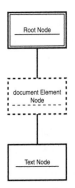

Figure 9.1 A representation of an XML document as an XPath hierarchy.

In this short example document, only three nodes are shown as representing the document. The root node is at the apex of the hierarchy. It has one child node: the document element node. Notice that there is no node to represent the XML declaration in our document. The XPath 1.0 data model has no representation for the XML declaration or for the DOCTYPE declaration.

> **Note**   In XPath, element nodes and attribute nodes have names that correspond to the element type name and attribute name. Not all XPath node types have names.

The document element node has a single text node as its only child node. The value of the text node is the text string George Bush is the son of George Bush, which is the content of the document element.

A full representation of the document would also include a namespace node, representing the implicit default XML namespace, whose namespace URI is http://www.w3.org/XML/1998/namespace.

XPath Axes

XPath is intended to allow a processor to navigate around the in-memory representation of an XML document. To describe how to navigate, it's necessary to express where that navigation starts and which direction(s) to take from that starting point—much like a set of street directions.

The starting point for navigation around a document using the XPath axes is called the *context node*. The context node can be the root node or any other node. A special form of syntax, beginning with the forward slash (/) character, indicates that the root node is the context node.

XPath processors navigate around the in-memory representation of an XML document by means of *axes*. Thirteen types of axes exist in XPath. Each axis represents a "direction" that the processor can take, beginning from the context node.

The following list briefly describes the XPath 1.0 axes. The child axis and attribute axis are the most frequently used and are considered in more detail later in this chapter.

> **Note** All axis names in XPath begin with lowercase letters.

- `child` axis—Contains the child nodes (including element nodes) of the context node

- `attribute` axis—When the context node is an element node, contains an attribute node for each attribute on the element

- `descendant` axis—Contains the child nodes of the context node, their child nodes, and so on

- `self` axis—Contains the context node itself

- `descendant-or-self` axis—Contains the nodes in both the `descendant` axis and the `self` axis

- `parent` axis—Contains the parent node of the context node

- `ancestor` axis—Contains the parent node of the context node (if it has one), that node's parent node, and so on

- `ancestor-or-self` axis—Contains the nodes in the `ancestor` axis for the context node and the `self` axis

- `namespace` axis—When the context node is an element node, contains a namespace node for each in-scope namespace declaration

- `following` axis—Contains nodes later in document order than the context node, excluding nodes in the `descendant` axis, `attribute` axis, or `namespace` axis

- `following-sibling` axis—Contains nodes in the `following` axis, but only if the nodes have the same parent node as the context node

- `preceding` axis—Contains nodes that occur earlier in document order than the context node, excluding nodes in the `ancestor` axis

- `preceding-sibling` axis—Contains nodes that satisfy the criteria for the preceding axis but that also have the same parent node as the context node

The Node Types in XPath 1.0

In XPath 1.0, seven types of node are specified, each of which corresponds to a structure in the source XML document:

- Root node—Represents the document entity

- Element node—Corresponds to an element in the source document

- Attribute node—Corresponds to an attribute in the source document

- Namespace node—Corresponds to each namespace declaration in scope for an element

- Processing instruction node—Corresponds to a processing instruction in the source document

- Comment node—Corresponds to a comment in the source document

- Text node—Corresponds to character content of an element in the source document

Each XPath axis has a *principal node type*. For the `attribute` axis, the principal node type is the attribute node. For the `namespace` axis, the principal node type is the namespace node. For all other axes, the principal node type is the element node.

Let's move on to consider how XPath expressions are written to define the axis that you plan to use and other parts of the expression.

XPath Syntax

In XPath, an *expression* is used to select nodes to be processed in a way appropriate to the application in which XPath is being used. The most commonly used type of XPath expression is the *location path* that returns a set of nodes, called a node-set.

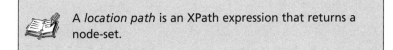

A *location path* is an XPath expression that returns a node-set.

XPath uses two forms of syntax for an expression: unabbreviated syntax and abbreviated syntax.

We will briefly use the unabbreviated syntax to demonstrate the general principles of XPath syntax. Mainly abbreviated syntax is used in the rest of the chapter.

Unabbreviated syntax for a location path takes the following general form if the context node is the root node:

```
/axisName::nodeTest[predicate]/axisName::nodeTest[predicate]
```

For other context nodes, this form is used:

```
axisName::nodeTest[predicate]/axisName::nodeTest[predicate]
```

Let's break down the first of the two forms into its component parts. When a location path begins with the forward slash character (/),that indicates that the context node is the root node. The next part of the location path is the *location step*:

```
axisName::nodeTest[predicate]
```

This location step follows the normal form for a location step—an axis name followed by a pair of colon characters as a separator (::), followed by a node test and, optionally, by one or more predicates contained in square brackets.

Then you see the / character as a separator between location steps and a second location step that follows the same form as the first. The axis name can be any of the 13 axes listed earlier in the chapter.

The node test can be a name or a wildcard. If the location step was as follows, this would select element nodes named `Document` present in the `child` axis:

```
child::Document
```

Alternatively, you could use a wildcard, `*`, and select all element nodes in the `child` axis by writing this:

```
child::*
```

The abbreviated syntax follows the same general structure as the unabbreviated syntax, but parts of the structure might not be explicitly expressed. For example, this location path

```
child::myElement
```

is equivalent to this in abbreviated syntax:

```
myElement
```

The `child` axis is essentially the default axis in XPath 1.0 and doesn't need to be expressed.

Similarly, if you want to select an `edition` attribute node, perhaps in code like this

```
<book edition="2nd">
```

you can use this unabbreviated syntax

```
attribute::edition
```

or this abbreviated syntax:

```
@edition
```

Here, the `@` character is equivalent to the `attribute` axis name plus the `::` separator.

The syntax of XPath bears similarities to the syntax of directory paths used in some operating systems. For example, consider this a document:

```
<myDocument>
 <myIntroduction>
  Some introduction content.
 </myIntroduction>
</myDocument>
```

You then could select the `myDocument` element node simply by writing this:

```
/myDocument
```

The preceding location path has a single location step. The `/` character indicates the root node. The following characters, `myDocument`, select all `myDocument` element nodes that are in the `child` axis of the root node. In this case, there is one `myDocument` element node that corresponds to the document element of the source document. No predicate is present in the location path.

As stated earlier, location paths may consist of multiple location steps. For example, you could write a location path to select the `myIntroduction` element node:

```
/myDocument/myIntroduction
```

Again, the initial `/` character indicates that the root node is the context node. The first location step, `myDocument`, selects the `child` axis implicitly. The node test selects only `myDocument` element nodes. There is no predicate. The second `/` character is a separator between node steps. The second location step, `myIntroduction`, implicitly selects the `child` axis and applies a node test that selects only `myIntroduction` element nodes. Again, there is no predicate.

Let's move on to look at some examples of selecting elements and attributes.

Accessing Elements

A common and important use of XPath involves being able to access elements—or, more precisely, element nodes. XPath provides ways to select element nodes either by their relationship to another node or by name.

Consider a source document of the following structure:

```
<report>
 <author>John Smith</author>
 <date>2002/12/19</date>
 <title>Safety Assessment for Greenland Tropical Tours</title>
 <chapter number="1">Some text</chapter>
 <chapter number="2">Some text</chapter>
 <chapter number="3">Some text</chapter>
 <appendix>Some appendix stuff</appendix>
</report>
```

You can select all the child element nodes of the report element node by the following XPath location path:

```
/report/*
```

The / at the beginning of the location path indicates that you are starting at the root node. Then you select any report element nodes that are children of the root node. The next / character is a separator of one location step from another. The * character is a wildcard that indicates any child element node.

In the example document, the root node has exactly one report element node child, which, in turn, has seven element node children. The node-set returned by the location path would contain seven element nodes—one author element node, one date element node, one title element node, three chapter element nodes, and an appendix element node.

Often you will want to select element nodes of a particular type. For example, if you wanted to select only title element nodes, you would simply incorporate the name of the desired type of element node in the location path:

```
/report/title
```

XPath would select only title element node children of report element node children of the root node.

The use of predicates when selecting elements is discussed later in this chapter when we look at some XPath functions.

Accessing Attributes

Selecting attributes is another important use of XPath. You learned earlier that you can use the @ character as an abbreviation for attribute::. You can use the following short XML document to illustrate how to select attributes.

```
<book edition="1st" language="English">
<introduction>Some introduction text</introduction>
<chapter number="1">
Some Chapter 1 text.
</chapter>
<chapter number="2">
Some Chapter 2 text.
</chapter>
<chapter >
Some Chapter 3 text.
</chapter>
<appendix designation="A">
Appendix A's content
</appendix>
</book>
```

If you want to select the edition attribute on the book element, you can write this:

```
/book/@edition
```

It might help you understand this to look at the unabbreviated form:

```
/child::book/attribute::edition
```

Start with the root node as context node (as indicated by the initial / character). Then follow the child axis and apply a node test of book. This selects book element nodes, of which there is exactly one in this document. Using the node-set selected by the first location step, you then follow the attribute axis from that single book element node and apply a node test of edition.

When you select the nodes in the attribute axis, two attribute nodes are selected: the edition and language attribute nodes. When you apply the edition node test to that node-set, only the edition attribute node matches. Thus, the location path selects a single attribute node corresponding to the `edition` attribute on the `book` element.

Now that you have seen how to select an attribute node, let's look at a way to select element nodes depending on the attribute node(s) that they possess. In the preceding example document, notice that the third `chapter` element has no `number` attribute. You can use that fact to select the first two `chapter` element nodes. The syntax to make that selection follows:

```
/book/chapter[@number]
```

The syntax `[@number]` is a predicate used to filter `chapter` element nodes. The part of the location path before the predicate selects element nodes named `chapter` that are child element nodes of the `book` element node. You then apply the predicate `[@number]` to the node-set that contains `chapter` element nodes. Only the first two `chapter` element nodes in document order possess `number` attribute nodes, so the third `chapter` element node (which has no `number` attribute node) is filtered out of the node-set.

On the other hand, if you wanted to select `number` attribute nodes on `chapter` element nodes, we could write this:

```
/book/chapter/@number
```

Follow the `child` axis from the root node to the single `book` element node and then the `child` axis to the `chapter` element nodes (of which there are three). Then, for each of the `chapter` element nodes, follow the `attribute` axis and apply a `number` node test. Only two of the `chapter` element nodes have a `number` attribute node, so only two `number` attribute nodes are selected.

XPath Functions

XPath provides a function library that can manipulate or return four data types—node-sets, Boolean values, strings, and numbers. This section briefly looks at how two of those functions can be used.

The `position()` Function

The `position()` function is widely used. Suppose that you have an XML document similar to the following:

```
<book>
<title>Sams Teach Yourself XML in 10 Minutes</title>
<chapter number="1" title="What is XML?">
<!-- The text of Chapter 1 could go here -->
</chapter>
<chapter number="2" title="The Structure of an XML document">
<!-- The text of Chapter 2 could go here -->
</chapter>
<!-- Other <chapter> elements and their content would go
  here -->
</book>
```

You might want to select the `chapter` element node that is second in document order. You can do that using the `position()` function by writing this:

```
/book/chapter[position()=2]
```

An abbreviated syntax exists for the `position()` function. The following syntax similarly selects the second `chapter` element node in document order:

```
/book/chapter[2]
```

The `count()` Function

Often it is useful to be able to count how many nodes are in a node-set. The `count()` function can be used to do that.

For example, suppose that you wanted to offer special offers to customers who had placed more than four orders with the company. Imagine that you store information about orders in a format similar to the following:

```
<customer CustID="DEF876">
<customerName>Greenland Tropical Tours</customerName>
<orders>
<order date="2001/12/22">
```

```
<!-- Order details would go here. -->
</order>
<order date="2002/01/31">
<!-- Order details would go here. -->
</order>
<order date="2002/07/16">
<!-- Order details would go here. -->
</order>
<!-- More <order> elements can go here. -->
</orders>
</customer>
```

You could count the number of order element nodes using the count()
function in the following XPath expression:

```
/customer/orders/count(order)
```

This would return a number that you could use, for example, in construct-
ing a table in HTML, if you used the XPath expression in an XSLT
stylesheet.

Many other XPath functions exist that cannot be described in the space
available here.

Summary

In this chapter, you were introduced to the XPath model of an XML document as a hierarchy of nodes. The node types were described, and the
abbreviated XPath syntax to select elements and attributes was discussed.
The chapter also gave some examples of widely used XPath functions.

LESSON 10

XSLT— Creating HTML from XML

In this lesson, you will learn how to use the Extensible Stylesheet Language Transformations (XSLT) to create HTML documents from data stored as XML.

XSLT Basics

XSLT is designed to be used with XML documents to *transform* data into a form appropriate for presentation in a particular context or into an alternate XML structure. In this chapter, you examine the basics of how to use XSLT to create HTML documents.

The output from an XSLT transformation can be another XML format (this is discussed in Chapter 11, "XSLT—Transforming XML Structure"), HTML documents (the main subject of this chapter), or plain text (not discussed in this book).

Why XSLT Is Needed

XML was originally intended to be transmitted across the Web, but since XML 1.0 was finalized in 1998, the implementation of XML in Web browsers has been slow and patchy. XML's failure to take over the Web browser does not mean that it is of no use as a data storage medium for the Web; however, at least for now, XML must be transformed into formats that are convenient for most Web users if XML data is to be available to them. That means that you need to be able to create HTML documents from XML data stores.

XSLT is ideally suited to creating HTML documents from XML server-side with the HTML produced being processed by a user's Web browser in the normal way. XSLT has an output mode to enable HTML output to be specified. In addition, XSLT can be used to produce HTML for desktop browsers, and Wireless Markup Language (WML) for mobile browsers from the same XML data store.

XSLT Tools

A large and growing number of XSLT tools is available. Appendix B, "XML Tools," lists some commonly used XSLT tools together with URLs where they can be downloaded. Appendix B also contains information about how to install these tools.

The examples in this chapter and the following two chapters illustrate the use of XSLT using the Instant Saxon XSLT processor.

A Basic XSLT Stylesheet

All XSLT stylesheets have either a `stylesheet` element or a `transform` element as their document element. Many stylesheet authors find it helpful to express XSLT elements with a namespace prefix of `xsl`, which is the indicative namespace prefix used in the XSLT 1.0 Recommendation.

XSLT elements in an XSLT stylesheet must be explicitly declared as belonging to the XSLT namespace. The XSLT namespace URI is `http://www.w3.org/1999/XSL/Transform`. Thus, a stylesheet will have either of the following basic structures, assuming that the namespace prefix `xsl` is declared as being associated with the XSLT namespace:

```
<?xml version="1.0" ?>
<xsl:stylesheet
xmlns:xsl="http://www.w3.org/1999/XSL/Transform
version="1.0">
<!-- The other XSLT elements and the literal result elements
  go here. -->
</xsl:stylesheet>
```

or

```
<?xml version="1.0" ?>
<xsl:transform
xmlns:xsl="http://www.w3.org/1999/XSL/Transform
version="1.0">
<!-- The other XSLT elements and the literal result elements
go here. -->
</xsl:transform>
```

Note The xsl:stylesheet or xsl:transform element must possess a version attribute. In XSLT 1.0, the only permitted value for the version attribute is 1.0.

Notice the XML declaration in both versions. All XSLT stylesheets are XML documents and, therefore, must follow all the well-formedness rules described earlier in Chapter 2, "The Structure of an XML Document," and Chapter 3, "XML Must Be Well-Formed."

The Structure of an XSLT Stylesheet

The xsl:stylesheet element is allowed to have only certain specified XSLT elements as its children. These are referred to, a little confusingly (because they are second-level elements), as *top-level elements*. The top-level elements are shown in the following list. If an xsl:import element is present, it must come before top-level elements of any other type. Apart from that, the ordering of top-level elements is open to the developer's preferences.

- xsl:import—Imports the content of one stylesheet (module) into the stylesheet containing the xsl:import element

- xsl:include—Includes the content of one stylesheet (module) in the stylesheet containing the xsl:include element

- xsl:template—Defines an XSLT template

- xsl:output—Defines parameters of the output document

- `xsl:attribute-set`—Used to define a named set of attributes

- `xsl:decimal-format`—Used in relation to the `format-number()` function

- `xsl:key`—Declares a named key to be used in relation to the `key()` function

- `xsl:namespace-alias`—Enables an XSLT stylesheet to be used to output another XSLT stylesheet as its result document

- `xsl:param`—(When a top-level element) Specifies a global parameter

- `xsl:preserve-space`—Controls whitespace handling in conjunction with `xsl:strip-space`

- `xsl:strip-space`—Controls whitespace handling in conjunction with `xsl:preserve-space`

- `xsl:variable`—(When a top-level element) Defines a global variable

Other XSLT elements are introduced as you meet them in the examples in this chapter and in Chapter 11 and Chapter 12, "XSLT—Sorting XML."

Having taken a brief look at the basics of what an XSLT stylesheet contains, let's move on to look at how to create an HTML Web page as the output of an XSLT transformation.

Creating a Simple HTML Page

It is traditional in many introductory programming texts to create a program that provides a "Hello World!" greeting.

Listing 10.1 shows a very short XML document that stores the message.

LISTING 10.1   XSLTMessage.xml: A Simple Message in XML

```
<?xml version='1.0'?>
<XSLTMessage>
Hello World!
</XSLTMessage>
```

You can use the XSLT stylesheet shown in Listing 10.2 to create an HTML Web page that extracts the message from Listing 10.1 and places it in the HTML page.

LISTING 10.2   XSLTMessage.xsl: A Stylesheet to Extract the Message from Listing 10.1

```
<?xml version='1.0'?>
<xsl:stylesheet
        xmlns:xsl="http://www.w3.org/1999/XSL/Transform"
        version="1.0"
  >

<xsl:template match="/">
<html>
<head>
<title><xsl:value-of select="name(/XSLTMessage)" /></title>
</head>
<body>
<xsl:apply-templates select="/XSLTMessage" />
</body>
</html>
</xsl:template>

<xsl:template match="XSLTMessage">
<p><xsl:value-of select="text()" /></p>
</xsl:template>
</xsl:stylesheet>
```

Before looking at the HTML output document that you can create, let's analyze what the XSLT stylesheet does.

The first line is an XML declaration. That is followed by the xsl:stylesheet element. It has a version attribute, which is compulsory, and a namespace declaration that associates the namespace prefix xsl with the XSLT namespace URI, http://www.w3.org/1999/XSL/Transform. So, it is clear that the xsl:stylesheet element and the other elements in the stylesheet with a namespace prefix xsl are XSLT elements.

When an XSLT processor is satisfied that a document is a well-formed XSLT stylesheet, it looks for an xsl:template element whose match attribute has a value of /. In other words, the template is applied to the root node.

Let's look at the content of that `xsl:template` element a little more closely:

```
<xsl:template match="/">
<html>
<head>
<title><xsl:value-of select="name(/XSLTMessage)" /></title>
</head>
<body>
<xsl:apply-templates select="/XSLTMessage" />
</body>
</html>
</xsl:template>
```

The first two lines nested within the `xsl:template` element contain *literal result elements*. In other words, you create an `html` start tag followed by `head` and `title` start tags. The content of the `title` element is defined using an XSLT `xsl:value-of` element, which you will use in many of your XSLT stylesheets. One question immediately arises: "The value of what?" That is answered by the value of the `select` attribute of the `xsl:value-of` element.

In this case, the value of the select attribute is this:

```
name(/XSLTMessage)
```

You use the `name()` function to extract the name of the document element. We have expressed that here by giving the element type name literally.

You then create the end tags for the `title` and `head` elements. Then you create the start tag for the `body` element.

The content of the body element is defined by the `xsl:apply-templates` element. Its `select` attribute indicates that a template that matches the context node defined by the XPath expression `/XSLTMessage` is to be instantiated.

```
<xsl:template match="XSLTMessage">
<p><xsl:value-of select="text()" /></p>
</xsl:template>
```

The only other template in the stylesheet matches the value in the `select` attribute of the `xsl:apply-templates` element. The content of that template defines the content of the body element of the HTML output document.

That content begins with a p start tag. It is followed by content defined by an xsl:value-of element. The value of the select attribute is text(); it selects the text node that is a child of the context node, which is the XSLTMessage element node. The template is completed by the creation of an end tag of the p element.

When that template is complete, you return to the template from which the template was instantiated. In other words, processing goes back to the template that matches the root node. Processing completes by outputting an end tag for the body and html elements—both literal result elements—of the HTML output document.

To run the transformation, assuming that Instant Saxon and Listings 10.1 and 10.2 are in the same directory, simply navigate to that directory and type this:

```
saxon XSLTMessage.xml XSLTMessage.xsl > XSLTMessage.html
```

Listing 10.3 shows the HTML document output by the Instant Saxon XSLT processor.

LISTING 10.3   XSLTMessage.html: The Output of Applying Listing 10.2 to Listing 10.1

```
<html>
 <head>
  <meta http-equiv="Content-Type" content="text/html;
   charset=utf-8">
  <title>XSLTMessage</title>
 </head>
 <body>
  <p>
   Hello World!
  </p>
 </body>
</html>
```

The Instant Saxon processor has added a meta element to the head of the HTML document.

If you plan to regularly create HTML documents using XSLT, it is useful
to have an XSLT template specific to HTML and save some repeated typing. Listing 10.4 gives a bare outline template that you might want to
adapt to your own needs.

LISTING 10.4   HTMLTemplate.xsl: An XSLT Stylesheet to
Create a Basic HTML Document

```
<?xml version='1.0'?>
<xsl:stylesheet
          xmlns:xsl="http://www.w3.org/1999/XSL/Transform"
  >
<xsl:output method="html"
 indent="yes" />
<xsl:template match="/">
<html>
<head>
<title><!--title goes here--></title>
</head>
<body>
<!-- XSLT code to create page content goes here. -->
</body>
</html>
</xsl:template>

</xsl:stylesheet>
```

If you routinely want to include metadata about the author of the HTML
document, its keywords, and so on, you can add those to the section that
creates the head of the HTML document.

Creating an HTML List

This section looks at how to create an HTML list from an XML source
document.

The XML source document contains information about a series of reports
produced for XMML.com. In this HTML Web page, you will choose to
display only reports for which the year of the report is 2002. Listing 10.5
shows the source XML document.

LISTING 10.5   XMMLReports.xml: Reports Presented to
XMML.com

```
<?xml version='1.0'?>
<XMMLReports>
<Report year="2000">
<Title>Sales Opportunities</Title>
<Author>Peter Mallan</Author>
<Summary>The opportunities for XML consultancy look good for
 2001.</Summary>
<Content>
<!-- Main text would go here. -->
</Content>
</Report>
<Report year="2001">
<Title>SVG - A Graphics Standard</Title>
<Author>Pamela Askew</Author>
<Summary>Scalable Vector Graphics, SVG, looks to have enormous
 potential in multinamespace XML documents.</Summary>
<Content>
<!-- Main text would go here. -->
</Content>
</Report>
<Report year="2002">
<Title>Market Conditions</Title>
<Author>Stephen J. Doppelganger</Author>
<Summary>Market conditions are much less favorable than in
 2001.</Summary>
<Content>
<!-- Main text would go here. -->
</Content>
</Report>
<Report year="2002">
<Title>XML Schema Languages</Title>
<Author>Karen Clark</Author>
<Summary>W3C XML Schema and RelaxNG both have positive
 aspects.</Summary>
<Content>
<!-- Main text would go here. -->
</Content>
</Report>
</XMMLReports>
```

Listing 10.6 shows the XSLT stylesheet that selects for display reports dated 2002 and displays the title, year, and author name for each such report.

LISTING 10.6   XMMLReports.xsl: A Stylesheet to Display Year 2002 Reports

```
<?xml version='1.0'?>
<xsl:stylesheet
 version="1.0"
 xmlns:xsl="http://www.w3.org/1999/XSL/Transform"
 >
<xsl:output method="html"
 indent="yes" />
<xsl:template match="/">
<html>
<head>
<title></title>
</head>
<body>
<h1>XMML.com Reports for 2002</h1>
<ul>
<xsl:apply-templates select="//Report[@year='2002']" />
</ul>
</body>
</html>
</xsl:template>

<xsl:template match="Report">
<li>
<xsl:value-of select="Title" />(<xsl:value-of
   select="@year"/>):<xsl:text>
</xsl:text><xsl:value-of select="Author" />
</li>
</xsl:template>

</xsl:stylesheet>
```

The preceding stylesheet bears many similarities to those you saw earlier in this chapter.

Notice the xsl:apply-templates element in the template that matches the root node. It is nested between the start and end tags of a ul element. So, the xsl:apply-templates element is used to create the content of the unordered list. The value of its select attribute is

//Report[@year='2002']. The pair of forward slash characters (*//*) is abbreviated syntax for the descendant-or-self axis. Essentially, *//Report* means to select any Report element node in the document. The predicate [@year='2002'] filters that node-set so that it includes only Report element nodes that possess a year attribute whose value is 2002.

The XSLT template that matches the nodes in that node-set is then processed. The xsl:template element with the match attribute whose value is Report is instantiated. A list item element, li, is created. The xsl:value-of element is used three times:

```
<xsl:value-of select="Title" />(<xsl:value-of
  select="@year"/>):<xsl:text> </xsl:text>
<xsl:value-of select="Author" />
```

First, the text content of the Title element is obtained, followed by the value of the year attribute of the Report element in parentheses. The third xsl:value-of element selects the text content of the Author element node for the report.

The xsl:text element is used to insert whitespace—in this case, a single space character—between the colon character and the author's name. Using the xsl:text element to output whitespace ensures that it is preserved in the output document.

The output of the transformation is shown in Listing 10.7.

LISTING 10.7 XMMLReports.html: The Output of Applying Listing 10.6 to Listing 10.5

```
<html>
 <head>
  <meta http-equiv="Content-Type" content="text/html;
   charset=utf-8">
  <title></title>
 </head>
 <body>
  <h1>XMML.com Reports for 2002</h1>
   <ul>
    <li>Market Conditions(2002): Stephen J. Doppelganger</li>
    <li>XML Schema Languages(2002): Karen Clark</li>
   </ul>
 </body>
</html>
```

Creating an HTML Table

In the final example in this chapter, you create an HTML table in the output document.

In this example, you look at how information about major news items stored in XML can be transformed using XSLT to produce an HTML page with links to the full news items. The structure of the source XML document is shown in Listing 10.8.

LISTING 10.8   XMMLNews.xml: An XML-Based Data Store Containing News Information

```
<?xml version='1.0'?>
<XMMLNews>
<Story>
<Headline>Teddy Bear's Picnic a Success</Headline>
<Header>2002 Teddy Bear's Picnic a great success.</Header>
<MainText>The Drum Castle (http://www.drum-castle.org.uk)
   Teddy Bear's Picnic for 2002 was a great success.
   etc</MainText>
</Story>
<Story>
<Headline>Snow Falls in Antarctica</Headline>
<Header>Heavy snow falls reported in Antarctica.</Header>
<MainText>The first snows of the Antarctic winter fell
   yesterday.</MainText>
</Story>
<Story>
<Headline>Brazil Win Cup.</Headline>
<Header>The Brazilian soccer team won the 2002 World
   Cup.</Header>
<MainText>After an exciting game, Brazil confirmed their
   dominance of world soccer with a convincing win.</MainText>
</Story>
</XMMLNews>
```

The number of stories and the components parts of each story have been kept short to save space.

The aim is to use XSLT to create an HTML Web page with a table, with each item in the table having a link to the full text of the story. Listing 10.9 shows a stylesheet that can produce the desired HTML Web page.

LISTING 10.9   XMMLNews.xsl: A Stylesheet to Produce a List of Stories in HTML

```
<?xml version='1.0'?>
<xsl:stylesheet
  version="1.0"
  xmlns:xsl="http://www.w3.org/1999/XSL/Transform"
  >
<xsl:output method="html"
  indent="yes" />
<xsl:template match="/">
<html>
<head>
<title>XMMLNews - Latest Stories</title>
</head>
<body>
<h1>XMML News Service</h1>
<table>
<tr>
<td><b>Headline</b></td>
<td><b>Main Text</b></td>
</tr>
<xsl:apply-templates select="/XMMLNews/Story"/>
</table>
</body>
</html>
</xsl:template>

<xsl:template match="Story" >
<tr>
<td><xsl:value-of select="Headline" /></td>
<td><xsl:value-of select='MainText'/></td>
</tr>
</xsl:template>

</xsl:stylesheet>
```

The HTML document output is shown in Listing 10.10.

LISTING 10.10   XMMLNews.html: A Table of Headlines and Stories

```
<html>
 <head>
  <meta http-equiv="Content-Type" content="text/html;
   charset=utf-8">
```

LISTING 10.10   Continued

```
 <title>XMMLNews - Latest Stories</title>
 </head>
 <body>
  <h1>XMML News Service</h1>
   <table>
    <tr>
     <td><b>Headline</b></td>
     <td><b>Main Text</b></td>
    </tr>
    <tr>
     <td>Teddy Bear's Picnic a Success</td>
     <td>The Drum Castle (http://www.drum-castle.org.uk) Teddy
        Bear's Picnic for 2002 was a great success. etc</td>
    </tr>
    <tr>
     <td>Snow Falls in Antarctica</td>
     <td>The first snows of the Antarctic winter fell
        yesterday.</td>
    </tr>
    <tr>
     <td>Brazil Win Cup.</td>
     <td>After an exciting game, Brazil confirmed their
        dominance of world soccer with a convincing win.</td>
    </tr>
   </table>
 </body>
</html>
```

Onscreen, the output is a basic HTML table.

Summary

In this lesson, you were introduced to the ways in which XSLT plays a valuable role in the current XML world. The structure of an XSLT stylesheet was described, and examples were given to show using XSLT to create several types of HTML pages, ranging from very basic on up to pages that include a list and a table.

LESSON 11

XSLT—
Transforming
XML Structure

*In this lesson, you will learn how to use XSLT to restructure content in
XML documents.*

Why Change Structure?

Chapter 8, "Namespaces in XML," mentioned problems that can occur
frequently as XML documents are exchanged among increasing numbers
of individuals and companies. XML namespaces do a lot to solve the
problem in which two identical element type names are used with different meanings. This chapter looks at how XSLT can be used to provide a
solution to the problem of different element type names being used to
refer to the same concept or real-world value. In addition, it looks more
generally at how XSLT can be used to restructure XML documents.

For example, one company might store an order like this, with date information in an element:

```
<order>
<date>2002-12-29</date>
<!-- More content here. -->
</order>
```

It might deal with a company that stores information about an order like
this, with date information stored in an attribute:

```
<order date="2002-12-29">
<!-- More content here. -->
</order>
```

When the companies exchange documents, the first company could send information in its own format. So, the second company would need to transform the XML so that the date element is removed and a date attribute is added to the order element. When the second company sends information back, the opposite process would need to be carried out.

Historically, companies and other organizations have had their own ways of describing the data that they use in the course of their business. When there was no direct exchange of data, that didn't matter too much. However, as businesses have started exchanging data—orders or shared information, for example—issues relating to the structure of that data have become increasingly important.

It would be pretty unusual for two companies to have identical data structures. But if both companies use XML to store their data, XSLT can be used to move from one format to another.

A number of possible solutions exist in any one setting. For example, each company could create an XSLT stylesheet to convert from the other company's data format. If a very small number of business partners are involved, that might work well. However, if a large number of companies in the same business sector work together, an alternate approach might be better.

If all the companies in the business sector can agree on a common data format for a particular type of data, each company needs only two XSLT stylesheets: one stylesheet to transform the company's format to the common format and another stylesheet to transform the common format to the company's format. It doesn't matter how large the number of business partners grows. If all use the common format, they don't need to add to the two stylesheets just mentioned.

Let's look at how transformations between formats can be carried out using XSLT. In the process of transforming XML documents from one structure to another, you need to be able to carry out three tasks:

- Copy elements from one document to another, possibly in a different part of the structure of the document

- Create new elements (for example when a value is contained in an attribute value in the source document and you need an element in the output document)

- Create new attributes (for example, when a value is contained in text element content in the source document and you need an attribute to contain the value in the output document)

First, let's look at how you can copy elements from one document to another.

Copying Elements

When you copy elements from one XML document to another, you will likely place the element in a new place in the structure. Sometimes you will want to copy an element only (without any child elements); other times, you might want to copy an element together with any content that it has. The first type of copy is called a *shallow copy*, and the second type is called a *deep copy*.

Shallow Copy

In XSLT, a shallow copy is carried out using the xsl:copy element. Listing 11.1 shows a simple purchase order for training services.

LISTING 11.1 PurchaseOrder.xml: A Purchase Order in XML

```
<?xml version='1.0'?>
<PurchaseOrder>
 <Date>2003/02/20</Date>
 <To>XMML Training Services</To>
 <From>Acme Computing</From>
 <Items>
  <Item>
   <StockNumber>DBI99</StockNumber>
   <Description>Database Introduction</Description>
   <Quantity>2</Quantity>
  </Item>
  <Item>
   <StockNumber>MSVG101</StockNumber>
```

LISTING 11.1   Continued

```
    <Description>Introduction to Mobile SVG</Description>
    <Quantity>1</Quantity>
    </Item>
  </Items>
</PurchaseOrder>
```

When such an XML purchase order is sent to XMML Training Services, the data contained in it can be reused for purposes of the receiving business partner. Listing 11.2 shows a stylesheet to convert the purchase order for the purposes of the recipient. The xsl:copy element is used in this transformation.

LISTING 11.2   PurchaseToOrder.xsl: An XSLT Stylesheet to Create an XML Order Received File

```
<?xml version='1.0'?>
<xsl:stylesheet
 version="1.0"
 xmlns:xsl="http://www.w3.org/1999/XSL/Transform"
 >

<xsl:template match="/">
<XMMLOrder>
<xsl:apply-templates select="/PurchaseOrder/Date" />
<xsl:apply-templates select="/PurchaseOrder/From" />
<xsl:apply-templates select="/PurchaseOrder/Items" />
</XMMLOrder>
</xsl:template>

<xsl:template match="Date|From">
<xsl:copy>
<xsl:value-of select="." />
</xsl:copy>
</xsl:template>

<xsl:template match="Items">
<xsl:copy>
<xsl:value-of select="." />
</xsl:copy>
</xsl:template>

</xsl:stylesheet>
```

This stylesheet takes you only part way to the desired output, as you can see by examining the content of the output document in Listing 11.3.

LISTING 11.3   XMMLOrder.xml: The Result of Applying Listing 11.2 to Listing 11.1

```
<?xml version="1.0" encoding="UTF-8"?>
<XMMLOrder>
    <Date>2003/02/20</Date>
    <From>Acme Computing</From>
    <Items>

    DBI99
    Database Introduction
    2


    MSVG101
    Introduction to Mobile SVG
    1

    </Items>
</XMMLOrder>
```

You have copied across the element node and, for the `Date` and `From` element nodes, included the element's content using the `xsl:value-of` element. So far, so good. However, when you use the `xsl:value-of` element with `xsl:copy` for the `Items` element node, you output only the text content of its descendant elements—but without outputting the corresponding start and end tags of the `Item` element and its child elements.

As you have seen, the `xsl:copy` element produces a shallow copy. You supply the content of the copied element by using the `xsl:value-of` element.

To correctly output and copy all the content of the `Items` element node, including the start and end tags of the descendant elements, you need to carry out a deep copy.

Deep Copy

The `xsl:copy-of` element is used in XSLT to carry out a deep copy.

Listing 11.4 shows an XSLT stylesheet that carries out the desired transformation. In this case, however, it uses the `xsl:copy-of` element in place of the `xsl:copy` element used in Listing 11.3.

LISTING 11.4   PurchaseToOrder2.xsl: Using `xsl:copy-of` to Produce a Deep Copy

```
<?xml version='1.0'?>
<xsl:stylesheet
 version="1.0"
 xmlns:xsl="http://www.w3.org/1999/XSL/Transform"
 >
<xsl:output method="xml"
 indent="yes"
 encoding="UTF-8" />
<xsl:template match="/">
<XMMLOrder>
<xsl:apply-templates select="/PurchaseOrder/Date" />
<xsl:apply-templates select="/PurchaseOrder/From" />
<xsl:apply-templates select="/PurchaseOrder/Items" />
</XMMLOrder>
</xsl:template>

<xsl:template match="Date|From">
<xsl:copy-of select="."/>
</xsl:template>

<xsl:template match="Items">
<xsl:copy-of select="." />
</xsl:template>

</xsl:stylesheet>
```

In Listing 11.4, the `xsl:copy` elements have been replaced with `xsl:copy-of` elements, which have a `select` attribute that selects the content of the context node. As you can see in Listing 11.5, the output of the transformation, using the `xsl:copy-of` element gives the text content of the Date and From elements and also gives the full hierarchy of elements and their content contained within the Items element.

LISTING 11.5   XMMLOrder2.xml: The Results Document
After Applying Listing 11.4 to Listing 11.1

```xml
<?xml version="1.0" encoding="UTF-8"?>
<XMMLOrder>
  <Date>2003/02/20</Date>
  <From>Acme Computing</From>
  <Items>

    <Item>

      <StockNumber>DBI99</StockNumber>

      <Description>Database Introduction</Description>

      <Quantity>2</Quantity>

    </Item>

    <Item>

      <StockNumber>MSVG101</StockNumber>

      <Description>Introduction to Mobile SVG</Description>

      <Quantity>1</Quantity>

    </Item>
  </Items>
</XMMLOrder>
```

In some transformations, you cannot simply copy elements from source
document to output document because there is some fundamental change
in structure. Often you will need to create new elements or attributes in
the output document. First let's look at how to create new elements.

Creating New Elements

In this section, you will look at two reasons why you might need to create
new elements.

In some transformations, the element names in the source document and the corresponding element name in the output document differ. For example, suppose that a company based in the United States is doing business with a company based in the United Kingdom. The U.S. company wants to place an order for white shirts. In the United States, the company might describe a white shirt, using this:

```
<Color>white</Color>
```

The U.K. company might use this line, however:

```
<Colour>white</Colour>
```

Only one letter is different in the element type name, but that is enough to trip up an XML parser.

Consider also that you might want to create a new element in the output document if the source document uses an attribute to store data that needs to be contained in an element in the output document. One company could have this

```
<Shirt size="medium"/>
```

and want to share the information with a company that stores data like this:

```
<Shirt>
<Size>medium</Size>
</Shirt>
```

You can explore both issues in Listing 11.6. The U.S. company uses a Color element that stores information about the color of the shirt. Because of differences in spelling, this information is held in a Colour element in the U.K. company's data store. Also, the U.K. company stores shirt size information in a Size element.

LISTING 11.6   USShirts.xml: An Order for Shirts from a Company Based in the United States

```
<?xml version='1.0'?>
<USShirts>
<Order>
<Date>2003/12/13</Date>
```

LISTING 11.6   Continued

```
<From>US Shirt Company</From>
<To>UK Shirt Company</To>
<Shirt size="medium">
<Color>Cerise</Color>
<Quantity>100</Quantity>
</Shirt>
</Order>
</USShirts>
```

Listing 11.7 shows the type of output document required. Notice the new Colour element and the Size element. In fact, Listing 11.7 is the result of applying the stylesheet in Listing 11.8 to Listing 11.6.

LISTING 11.7   UKShirts.xml: The U.K. Company's Form of XML for the Order

```
<?xml version="1.0" encoding="UTF-8"?>
<UKShirts>
    <Date>2003/12/13</Date>
    <From>US Shirt Company</From>
    <To>UK Shirt Company</To>
    <Shirt>
        <Size>Medium</Size>
        <Colour>Cerise</Colour>
        <Quantity>100</Quantity>
    </Shirt>
</UKShirts>
```

Notice that the Shirt element no longer has a size attribute; instead, it has a Size element child.

Listing 11.8 shows an XSLT stylesheet that creates two new elements using the xsl:element element. One of the new elements replaces a Color element with a Colour element. The other replaces a size attribute with a Size element.

LISTING 11.8   USShirtToUK.xsl: An XSLT Stylesheet to Transform to the U.K. Company's Data Structure

```
<?xml version='1.0'?>
<xsl:stylesheet
    version="1.0"
```

LISTING 11.8 Continued

```
xmlns:xsl="http://www.w3.org/1999/XSL/Transform"
>
<xsl:output method="xml" indent="yes" encoding="UTF-8" />
<xsl:template match="/">
<UKShirts>
<xsl:apply-templates select="/USShirts/Order" />
</UKShirts>
</xsl:template>

<xsl:template match="Order" >
<xsl:apply-templates select="Date" />
<xsl:apply-templates select="From" />
<xsl:apply-templates select="To" />
<xsl:apply-templates select="Shirt" />
</xsl:template>

<xsl:template match="Date" >
<xsl:copy-of select="." />
</xsl:template>

<xsl:template match="From|To" >
<xsl:copy-of select="." />
</xsl:template>

<xsl:template match="Shirt">
<xsl:copy>
<xsl:element name="Size">
<xsl:value-of select="@size" />
</xsl:element>
<xsl:apply-templates select="Color" />
<xsl:apply-templates select="Quantity" />
</xsl:copy>
</xsl:template>

<xsl:template match="Color">
<xsl:element name="Colour">
<xsl:value-of select="." />
</xsl:element>
</xsl:template>

<xsl:template match="Quantity">
<xsl:copy-of select="." />
</xsl:template>

</xsl:stylesheet>
```

The `xsl:element` element is used in two templates in the XSLT
stylesheet.

```
<xsl:template match="Shirt">
<xsl:copy>
<xsl:element name="Size">
<xsl:value-of select="@size" />
</xsl:element>
<xsl:apply-templates select="Color" />
<xsl:apply-templates select="Quantity" />
</xsl:copy>
</xsl:template>
```

First, you use `xsl:copy` to create a shallow copy of the `Shirt` element.
Because you have used a shallow copy, that leaves you free to create new
content for that element. You use the `xsl:element` element to create a new
element—the `Size` element—to contain the content of the `size` attribute.
Notice that the `name` attribute of the `xsl:element` element is the same as
the element type name of the element you are creating.

The `xsl:apply-templates` element instantiates a template that matches
the `Color` element:

```
<xsl:template match="Color">
<xsl:element name="Colour">
<xsl:value-of select="." />
</xsl:element>
</xsl:template>
```

Here the `xsl:element` is used to create a new `Colour` element (U.K.
spelling) to replace the `Color` element (U.S. spelling). The content of the
new element is identical to the content of the `Color` element, so you can
simply use the `xsl:value-of` element to select the text content of the
`Color` element as the content of the new `Colour` element.

By using the `xsl:copy`, `xsl:copy-of`, and `xsl:element` elements, you
have been able to transform from the U.S. data format to the format
desired by the U.K. company.

However, if you want to transform the data from the U.K. format to the
U.S. format, you need to learn how to create new attributes.

Creating New Attributes

To create a new attribute in the output document, you need to use the xsl:attribute element.

On this occasion, you will transform a source document in the U.K. company's format to an XML output document in the U.S. company's format. Listing 11.9 shows an XSLT stylesheet that can carry out the transformation.

LISTING 11.9   UKShirtsToUS.xsl: An XSLT Stylesheet to Transform to the U.S. Company's Data Format

```
<?xml version='1.0'?>
<xsl:stylesheet
 version="1.0"
 xmlns:xsl="http://www.w3.org/1999/XSL/Transform"
 >
<xsl:output method="xml" indent="yes" encoding="UTF-8" />
<xsl:template match="/">
<USShirts>
<Order>
<xsl:apply-templates select="/UKShirts" />
</Order>
</USShirts>
</xsl:template>

<xsl:template match="Order" >
<xsl:apply-templates select="Date" />
<xsl:apply-templates select="From" />
<xsl:apply-templates select="To" />
<xsl:apply-templates select="Shirt" />
</xsl:template>

<xsl:template match="Date" >
<xsl:copy-of select="." />
</xsl:template>

<xsl:template match="From|To" >
<xsl:copy-of select="." />
</xsl:template>

<xsl:template match="Shirt">
<xsl:copy>
```

LISTING 11.9   Continued

```
<xsl:attribute name="size">
<xsl:value-of select="Size" />
</xsl:attribute>
<xsl:apply-templates select="Colour" />
<xsl:apply-templates select="Quantity" />
</xsl:copy>
</xsl:template>

<xsl:template match="Colour">
<xsl:element name="Color">
<xsl:value-of select="." />
</xsl:element>
</xsl:template>

<xsl:template match="Quantity">
<xsl:copy-of select="." />
</xsl:template>

</xsl:stylesheet>
```

Use the xsl:attribute in the template that matches the Shirt element node:

```
<xsl:template match="Shirt">
<xsl:copy>
<xsl:attribute name="size">
<xsl:value-of select="Size" />
</xsl:attribute>
<xsl:apply-templates select="Colour" />
<xsl:apply-templates select="Quantity" />
</xsl:copy>
</xsl:template>
```

First copy the Shirt element using xsl:copy. Then use the xsl:attribute element to add an attribute to the Shirt element. The value of that new shirt attribute is obtained from the content of the Size element. The first xsl-apply-templates element is used to create a new Color element to replace the Colour element used by the U.K. company's format.

If you can carry out shallow and deep copies and create new elements and new attributes, you can accomplish many of the basic tasks that are necessary in converting one XML format to another.

Summary

In this lesson, you learned about the need to transform one XML vocabulary to another. You saw how to use the `xsl:copy` element to make a shallow copy and the `xsl:copy-of` element to make a deep copy of elements from the source document. You also saw how to create new elements using the `xsl:element` element and create new attributes in the output document using the `xsl:attribute` element.

LESSON 12
XSLT— Sorting XML

In this lesson, you will learn how to sort selected content to produce output documents sorted on one or multiple criteria.

Conditional Processing and Sorting Data

As you saw in Chapter 11, "XSLT—Transforming XML Structure," an XML document may not be in the precise form that you want to work with. In addition to providing tools to copy or to create new elements and attributes, XSLT provides tools to process data according to criteria that you set. Among the important functionality that XSLT provides is the capability to process elements (or not) based on criteria that you define or to sort data according to criteria that you specify.

Many programming languages have `if ... then ... else` statements or similar constructs. In XSLT, you can use the `xsl:if` element for similar purposes. For more complicated choices, conventional programming languages have a `switch/case` statement or similar construct. In XSLT, you can use the `xsl:choose` element to make choices when more than two options are involved.

Data stored in an XML document may be ordered according to some arbitrary criteria, perhaps as simple as the sequence in which elements and their content were first entered into the data store. For some purposes, you likely will want to use data in various orders—including alphabetical order, date order, and by value of element content or attribute value. XSLT possesses the `xsl:sort` element to provide sorting functionality.

First, let's look more closely at conditional processing and how it is supported in XSLT.

Conditional Processing

Controlling choices in XSLT as to how and whether a node is to be processed falls into two categories:

- Choice of two processing alternatives, one of which is to do nothing

- Choice of multiple (greater than two) options

The `xsl:if` Element

The `xsl:if` element in XSLT corresponds broadly to `if...then... else` type statements in other programming languages, but in XSLT there is no `else` option. If you want an `else` option, you must use `xsl:choose`, described later in this chapter.

An `xsl:if` element is always nested within an `xsl:template` element. XSLT elements that are nested within templates are termed *instructions* or *instruction elements*.

The general form is like this:

```
<xsl:template>
<!-- Other content can go here. -->
<xsl:if test="XPathExpression">
<!-- Anything in here is executed if the test attribute
 returns true. -->
</xsl:if>
<!-- Other content can go here. -->
</xsl:template>
```

The value of the `test` attribute is converted to a Boolean value. If the result is `true`, the content of the `xsl:if` element is instantiated. If the result is `false`, the content of the `xsl:if` element is skipped.

The following list summarizes the rules for conversion to Boolean values:

- If the expression is a node-set, the Boolean value true is returned if the node-set contains one or more nodes.

- If the expression is a number, the Boolean value returned is true if the number is not zero.

- If the expression is a string, the Boolean value returned is true if the string is not the empty string.

Some possible uses of xsl:if can be more succinctly expressed using a predicate.

For example, if you wanted to specify that a document was to be included in a results document only if a version attribute had the value final, you could use xsl:if inside a template that matched the Document element node:

```
<xsl:template match="Document">
<!-- All Document elements get to here. -->
<xsl:if test="@version='final'">
<!-- Conditional processing of final version documents only
     goes here. -->
</xsl:if>
<!-- Any other processing that applies to all Document element
     nodes could go here. -->
</xsl:template>
```

However, you could just as easily control things using a predicate [@version="final"] in the location path in an xsl:apply-templates element's select attribute.

However, when you want to process all Document element nodes but process them differently depending on whether they are final or draft, you can make use of the xsl:if element. Listing 12.1 shows an example XML source document.

Listing 12.1   Documents.xml: An XML Data Store
Containing Final and Draft Documents

```xml
<?xml version='1.0'?>
<Documents>
  <Document version="outdated">
    <Title>XMML.com Training Courses</Title>
    <Author>Karen Karenstein</Author>
    <Date>1999/12/20</Date>
    <Content>December 1999 content.</Content>
  </Document>
  <Document version="final">
    <Title>XMML.com Training Courses</Title>
    <Author>Camilla Zukowski</Author>
    <Date>2002/12/29</Date>
    <Content>December 2002 content.</Content>
  </Document>
  <Document version="draft">
    <Title>XMML.com Training Courses</Title>
    <Author>Camilla Zukowski</Author>
    <Date>2002/07/31</Date>
    <Content>July 2002 draft content.</Content>
  </Document>
  <Document version="final">
    <Title>XMML.com Consultancy Services</Title>
    <Author>Paul Hartington</Author>
    <Date>2003/04/29</Date>
    <Content>April 2003 consultancy services
    information.</Content>
  </Document>
</Documents>
```

Listing 12.2 is an XSLT stylesheet that outputs the information about
final version documents with a red h1 header and full information about
the document author, together with the document content. For documents
with a version attribute equal to draft or outdated, the document title is
output in an h2 element in blue and only the document status is output for
each such document.

Listing 12.2   Documents.xsl: An XSLT Stylesheet Using the
xsl:if Element

```xml
<?xml version='1.0'?>
<xsl:stylesheet
 version="1.0"
```

Listing 12.2 Continued

```
xmlns:xsl="http://www.w3.org/1999/XSL/Transform"
  >
<xsl:output method="html"
  indent="yes" />
<xsl:template match="/">
<html>
<head>
<title>XMML.com Documents</title>
<style type="text/css">
h2{color:red}
h3{color:blue}
</style>
</head>
<body>
<h1>All XMML.com documents.</h1>
<xsl:apply-templates select="//Document" />

</body>
</html>
</xsl:template>

<xsl:template match="Document">
<xsl:if test="@version='final'">
<h2>Document Title:<xsl:text> </xsl:text><xsl:value-of select=
  "Title" /></h2>
</xsl:if>
<xsl:if test="not(@version='final')">
<h3>Document Title:<xsl:text> </xsl:text><xsl:value-of select=
  "Title" /></h3>
</xsl:if>
<p>Document Status:<xsl:text> </xsl:text><xsl:value-of select=
  "@version"/></p>
<xsl:if test="@version='final'">
<p>Document Author:<xsl:text> </xsl:text><xsl:value-of select=
  "Author"/></p>
<p>Document Content:<xsl:text> </xsl:text><b><xsl:value-of
select=
  "Content"/></b></p>
</xsl:if>
</xsl:template>

</xsl:stylesheet>
```

Listing 12.3 contains the output from the XSLT transformation.

Listing 12.3   Documents.html: The Output Document
After Applying Listing 12.2 to Listing 12.1

```html
<html>
    <head>
        <meta http-equiv="Content-Type" content="text/html;
        charset=utf-8">

        <title>XMML.com Documents</title><style type="text/css">
h2{color:red}
h3{color:blue}
</style></head>
    <body>
        <h1>All XMML.com documents.</h1>
        <h3>Document Title: XMML.com Training Courses</h3>
        <p>Document Status: outdated</p>
        <h2>Document Title: XMML.com Training Courses</h2>
        <p>Document Status: final</p>
        <p>Document Author: Camilla Zukowski</p>
        <p>Document Content: <b>December 2002 content.</b></p>
        <h3>Document Title: XMML.com Training Courses</h3>
        <p>Document Status: draft</p>
        <h2>Document Title: XMML.com Consultancy Services</h2>
        <p>Document Status: final</p>
        <p>Document Author: Paul Hartington</p>
        <p>Document Content: <b>April 2003 consultancy services
            information. </b></p>
    </body>
</html>
```

Figure 12.1 shows Listing 12.3 displayed in the Internet Explorer 5.5
browser.

To use only `xsl:if` elements to achieve output like this can be a little
clumsy at times. Let's modify the output by using the `xsl:choose` element
in an XSLT transformation.

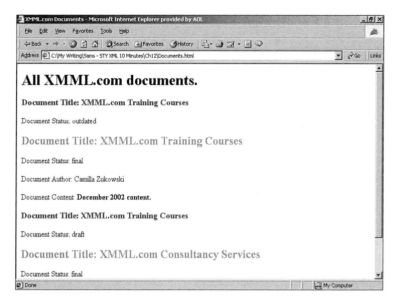

Figure 12.1   Differential display of documents depending on the value of the version attribute.

The `xsl:choose` Element

The `xsl:choose` element enables you to make multiple choices about how nodes should be processed. For each specified test, you use an `xsl:when` element with a `test` attribute. If you want to create a default type of processing when none of the tests on `xsl:when` elements is satisfied, you can use an `xsl:otherwise` element.

Listing 12.4 shows a modified stylesheet. When the value of the `version` attribute has the value `final`, you will output the full document as in the earlier example. This time, you will create different outputs when the value of the `version` attribute is `draft` or `outdated`.

Listing 12.4   Documents2.xsl: A Modified XSLT Stylesheet
Using `xsl:choose`

```
<?xml version='1.0'?>
<xsl:stylesheet
 version="1.0"
 xmlns:xsl="http://www.w3.org/1999/XSL/Transform"
 >
<xsl:output method="html"
 indent="yes" />
<xsl:template match="/">
<html>
<head>
<title>XMML.com Documents</title>
<style type="text/css">
h2{color:red}
h3{color:blue}
</style>
</head>
<body>
<h1>All XMML.com documents.</h1>
<xsl:apply-templates select="//Document" />

</body>
</html>
</xsl:template>

<xsl:template match="Document">
<xsl:choose>
<xsl:when test="@version='final'">
<h2>Document Title:<xsl:text> </xsl:text><xsl:value-of select=
  "Title" /></h2>
<p>Document Status:<xsl:text> </xsl:text><xsl:value-of select=
  "@version"/></p>
<p>Document Author:<xsl:text> </xsl:text><xsl:value-of select=
  "Author"/></p>
<p>Document Content:<xsl:text> </xsl:text><b><xsl:value-of
  select="Content"/></b></p>
</xsl:when>
<xsl:when test="@version='draft'">
<h3>Document Title:<xsl:text> </xsl:text><xsl:value-of select=
  "Title" /></h3>
<p>Document Status:<xsl:text> </xsl:text><xsl:value-of select=
  "@version"/></p>
</xsl:when>
```

Listing 12.4 Continued

```
<xsl:otherwise >
<!-- The version attribute is "outdated". -->
<!-- Do nothing -->
</xsl:otherwise>
</xsl:choose>
</xsl:template>

</xsl:stylesheet>
```

Two xsl:when elements are nested inside the xsl:choose element. The content of each xsl:when element is processed when a Document element satisfies the test in the test attribute of the xsl:when element.

Listing 12.5 shows the modified HTML output document. Notice that the outdated document does not appear in this output document because the xsl:otherwise element does nothing.

Listing 12.5 Documents2.html: The Output of the Stylesheet Using xsl:choose

```
<?xml version='1.0'?>
<xsl:stylesheet
 version="1.0"
 xmlns:xsl="http://www.w3.org/1999/XSL/Transform"
  >
<xsl:output method="html"
 indent="yes" />
<xsl:template match="/">
<html>
<head>
<title>XMML.com Documents</title>
<style type="text/css">
h2{color:red}
h3{color:blue}
</style>
</head>
<body>
<h1>All XMML.com documents.</h1>
<xsl:apply-templates select="//Document" />

</body>
</html>
</xsl:template>
```

Listing 12.5   Continued

```
<xsl:template match="Document">
<xsl:choose>
<xsl:when test="@version='final'">
<h2>Document Title:<xsl:text> </xsl:text><xsl:value-of select=
   "Title" /></h2>
<p>Document Status:<xsl:text> </xsl:text><xsl:value-of select=
   "@version"/></p>
<p>Document Author:<xsl:text> </xsl:text><xsl:value-of select=
   "Author"/></p>
<p>Document Content:<xsl:text> </xsl:text><b><xsl:value-of
   select="Content"/></b></p>
</xsl:when>
<xsl:when test="@version='draft'">
<h3>Document Title:<xsl:text> </xsl:text><xsl:value-of select=
   "Title" /></h3>
<p>Document Status:<xsl:text> </xsl:text><xsl:value-of select=
   "@version"/></p>
</xsl:when>
<xsl:otherwise >
<!-- The version attribute is "outdated". -->
<!-- Do nothing -->
</xsl:otherwise>
</xsl:choose>
</xsl:template>

</xsl:stylesheet>
```

The output of each type of document is not in any particular order—it merely reflects document order in Listing 12.1. In some situations, you would want to sort the order of elements in the output document.

Sorting Output

XSLT provides the xsl:sort element to enable you to sort output from a transformation into the order that you want. If you want to sort by two criteria, you can nest xsl:sort elements inside each other.

Listing 12.6 uses the xsl:sort element to output all documents that are final before those that are drafts. Outdated documents are governed by the xsl:otherwise element and are not output.

Listing 12.6   Documents3.xsl: Sorting Documents in Descending Alphabetical Order by version Attribute Value

```
<?xml version='1.0'?>
<xsl:stylesheet
  version="1.0"
  xmlns:xsl="http://www.w3.org/1999/XSL/Transform"
  >
<xsl:output method="html"
  indent="yes" />
<xsl:template match="/">
<html>
<head>
<title>XMML.com Documents</title>
<style type="text/css">
h2{color:red}
h3{color:blue}
</style>
</head>
<body>
<h1>All XMML.com documents.</h1>
<xsl:apply-templates select="//Document" >
<xsl:sort select="@version"
  order="descending"
  data-type="text"/>
</xsl:apply-templates>
</body>
</html>
</xsl:template>

<xsl:template match="Document">
<xsl:choose>
<xsl:when test="@version='final'">
<h2>Document Title:<xsl:text> </xsl:text><xsl:value-of select=
  "Title" /></h2>
<p>Document Status:<xsl:text> </xsl:text><xsl:value-of select=
  "@version"/></p>
<p>Document Author:<xsl:text> </xsl:text><xsl:value-of select=
  "Author"/></p>
<p>Document Content:<xsl:text> </xsl:text><b><xsl:value-of
  select="Content"/></b></p>
</xsl:when>
<xsl:when test="@version='draft'">
<h3>Document Title:<xsl:text> </xsl:text><xsl:value-of select=
  "Title" /></h3>
```

Listing 12.6   Continued

```
<p>Document Status:<xsl:text> </xsl:text><xsl:value-of select=
  "@version"/></p>
</xsl:when>
<xsl:otherwise >
<!-- The version attribute is "outdated". -->
<!-- Do nothing -->
</xsl:otherwise>
</xsl:choose>
</xsl:template>

</xsl:stylesheet>
```

The key change to the XSLT stylesheet is in the `xsl:apply-templates` element in the main template.

```
<xsl:apply-templates select="//Document" >
<xsl:sort select="@version"
 order="descending"
 data-type="text"/>
</xsl:apply-templates>
```

Instead of having an empty `xsl:apply-templates` element, an `xsl:sort` element is nested inside the `xsl:apply-templates` element. You specify the sort key using the `select` attribute. The order—ascending or descending—is specified using the `order` attribute. The data type—text, number, or QName—is specified using the `data-type` attribute.

Listing 12.7 shows the sorted output. The two documents that are final come before the single draft document because you are sorting in descending order and because final comes after draft alphabetically.

Listing 12.7   Documents3.html: Output Sorted by Value of the `version` Attribute

```
<html>
    <head>
        <meta http-equiv="Content-Type" content="text/html;
          charset=utf-8">

        <title>XMML.com Documents</title><style type="text/css">
h2{color:red}
h3{color:blue}
</style></head>
```

Listing 12.7 Continued

```
<body>
    <h1>All XMML.com documents.</h1>
    <h2>Document Title: XMML.com Training Courses</h2>
    <p>Document Status: final</p>
    <p>Document Author: Camilla Zukowski</p>
    <p>Document Content: <b>December 2002 content.</b></p>
    <h2>Document Title: XMML.com Consultancy Services</h2>
    <p>Document Status: final</p>
    <p>Document Author: Paul Hartington</p>
    <p>Document Content: <b>April 2003 consultancy services
        information. </b></p>
    <h3>Document Title: XMML.com Training Courses</h3>
    <p>Document Status: draft</p>
</body>
</html>
```

 Note The xsl:sort element can also be used with the xsl:for-each element. That usage is not considered in this book, however.

You can sort on more than one criterion using multiple xsl:sort elements.

Multiple Sorts

When you use multiple xsl:sort elements, you put the major sort criterion first, then the next most important, and so on if you are using more than two sort criteria.

The xsl:sort element must be a direct child element of the xsl:apply-templates element (in this example). It is an error to nest xsl:sort elements inside each other.

Listing 12.8 shows the XSLT stylesheet modified so that it outputs all (here, both) the final documents first, but those final documents are themselves sorted in ascending alphabetical order.

Listing 12.8   Documents4.xsl: Applying Two Sorts to the
Source Document

```xml
<?xml version='1.0'?>
<xsl:stylesheet
 version="1.0"
 xmlns:xsl="http://www.w3.org/1999/XSL/Transform"
 >
<xsl:output method="html"
 indent="yes" />
<xsl:template match="/">
<html>
<head>
<title>XMML.com Documents</title>
<style type="text/css">
h2{color:red}
h3{color:blue}
</style>
</head>
<body>
<h1>All XMML.com documents.</h1>
<xsl:apply-templates select="//Document" >
<xsl:sort select="@version"
 order="descending"
 data-type="text"/>
<xsl:sort select="Title"
  order="ascending"
  data-type="text"/>
</xsl:apply-templates>
</body>
</html>
</xsl:template>

<xsl:template match="Document">
<xsl:choose>
<xsl:when test="@version='final'">
<h2>Document Title:<xsl:text> </xsl:text><xsl:value-of select=
  "Title" /></h2>
<p>Document Status:<xsl:text> </xsl:text><xsl:value-of select=
  "@version"/></p>
<p>Document Author:<xsl:text> </xsl:text><xsl:value-of select=
  "Author"/></p>
<p>Document Content:<xsl:text> </xsl:text><b><xsl:value-of
  select="Content"/></b></p>
</xsl:when>
```

Listing 12.8   Continued

```
<xsl:when test="@version='draft'">
<h3>Document Title:<xsl:text> </xsl:text><xsl:value-of select=
   "Title" /></h3>
<p>Document Status:<xsl:text> </xsl:text><xsl:value-of select=
   "@version"/></p>
</xsl:when>
<xsl:otherwise >
<!-- The version attribute is "outdated". -->
<!-- Do nothing -->
</xsl:otherwise>
</xsl:choose>
</xsl:template>

</xsl:stylesheet>
```

Because "Consultancy Services" is alphabetically before "Training Services," the consultancy services document appears first in the output document, as you can see in Listing 12.9.

Listing 12.9   Documents4.html: The Output Document After Applying Listing 12.8

```
<html>
    <head>
        <meta http-equiv="Content-Type" content="text/html;
        charset=utf-8">

        <title>XMML.com Documents</title><style type="text/css">
h2{color:red}
h3{color:blue}
</style></head>
    <body>
        <h1>All XMML.com documents.</h1>
        <h2>Document Title: XMML.com Consultancy Services</h2>
        <p>Document Status: final</p>
        <p>Document Author: Paul Hartington</p>
        <p>Document Content: <b>April 2003 consultancy services
           information.</b></p>
        <h2>Document Title: XMML.com Training Courses</h2>
        <p>Document Status: final</p>
        <p>Document Author: Camilla Zukowski</p>
        <p>Document Content: <b>December 2002 content.</b></p>
```

Listing 12.9   Continued

```
      <h3>Document Title: XMML.com Training Courses</h3>
      <p>Document Status: draft</p>
   </body>
</html>
```

Summary

In this lesson, you were introduced to how the `xsl:if` and `xsl:choose` elements can be used to carry out conditional processing when transforming XML documents. In addition, you learned how to use the `xsl:sort` element to sort nodes according to single and multiple criteria.

LESSON 13
Styling XML with CSS

In this lesson, you will learn how to associate a Cascading Style Sheets (CSS) style sheet with an XML document and use CSS rules to style XML documents. Combining CSS and XSLT to style XML documents is also discussed and demonstrated.

Cascading Style Sheets and XML

Cascading Style Sheets (CSS) is a styling technology that uses non-XML syntax to style elements in markup languages such as HTML. It also is suitable for some tasks in the styling of XML.

CSS style sheets can be used on their own with XML or can be used with XML and XSLT. Both uses are described and illustrated in this lesson.

> **Note** In CSS, the words *style sheet* are two separate words. In XSLT, the term *stylesheet* is a single word. This difference in spelling arose because these of the separate initial development of these two technologies at W3C.

First let's look at some of the background that explains why CSS was invented and what problems it solves.

Separating Content and Presentation

Having a site-wide coherent visual appearance is desirable for all but the most anarchic Web sites. A coordinated style with good design characteristics can make a positive impression on visitors to a site. On that basis alone, it is useful to be able to easily create a style that applies across a whole Web site. But there were difficulties in doing that without CSS.

One of the problems with HTML—and one of the problems that led to the development of XML—was that content and presentation were intertwined. For example, an h1 element indicated a heading, but, almost inevitably, it also indicated a larger size for the contained text.

In the early days of HTML, it was common for the same person to create all aspects of an HTML Web page. The Web page creator carried out design tasks and content tasks pretty much seamlessly. When a page is created, and particularly when a site consists of a small number of pages, one-person authoring using HTML (with content and presentation intertwined) can work well. However, problems begin when a site grows and when it must be updated, perhaps by a different person and perhaps with a site-wide change in color or other style aspects. If style information is contained in HTML tags alone, updating style information in every individual page on a large site becomes a tedious, time-consuming, and expensive process.

Another factor that is increasingly relevant is that many Web pages, particularly on larger Web sites, are generated dynamically. If styling information was applied to each individual element in an HTML page created dynamically, the problems of updating potentially become even more severe. Any change in styling must be made within dynamically created HTML code contained, for example, in a Java servlet. This could mean even more time in amending styling information at potentially greater cost. Separating styling information for the site into a separate CSS stylesheet enables the Java code (or code in another language) to be shorter and more easily maintained.

Given these factors, a way obviously must be found to update styling information across a site efficiently, speedily, and not too expensively. By separating styling information into CSS style sheets, any necessary changes in content can be made independent of styling changes. Equally, styling can be changed without changing content or having to individually edit each HTML page. Taken together, these factors can save a lot of time and money in the ongoing costs of supporting a Web site.

Let's move on to look at how you can associate an external CSS style sheet with an XML document.

Associating a Stylesheet

The `xml-stylesheet` processing instruction is used to associate an XML document with a CSS style sheet or with an XSLT stylesheet of the type you saw in earlier chapters.

> **Tip** Place the `xml-stylesheet` processing instruction in the prolog of the XML document, in the line immediately after the XML declaration, if you used one.

The general form of the necessary processing instruction is as follows:

```
<?xml-stylesheet href="CSSStyleSheet.css" type="text/css" ?>
```

The second part of the `xml-stylesheet` processing instruction consists of two *pseudoattributes* (these aren't true attributes because they aren't associated with an element)—the `href` and `type` pseudoattributes.

An XML processor can use this information to recognize that there is a CSS file of type `text/css`, named *CSSStyleSheet.css*, which is associated with the XML document.

Using CSS Rules with XML

A CSS style sheet is made up of *rules*.

> A *rule* is the association of an element type name, a class, or other part of an XML document with a CSS declaration.

If an XML document includes a `title` element and you want the text content to be displayed at a font size of 24 points, you could write this:

```
title {font-size:24pt}
```

CSS Syntax

Whether it is internal (in a `style` element) or external, a CSS style sheet consists of rules. The following CSS rule associates the Arial font of size 36 with the `h1` element:

```
h1 {font-family:Arial, sans-serif;
font-size:36;}
```

The part of the rule outside the curly brackets is called a *selector*. Selectors can be grouped by separating them using commas. The following rule would apply to both `p` and `li` elements:

```
p, li {font-family:"Times Roman", serif;
font-size:12;}
```

A selector may consist of one or more element type names or may be more focused and include only certain elements that have a `class` attribute of a particular value. Imagine applying a rule to `p` elements with a `class` attribute with the value `confidential`:

```
<p class="confidential" ...>Some text<p>
```

To make the text red in color, you can use this rule:

```
p.confidential {color:#FF0000;}
```

The period in `p.confidential` separates the element type name, `p`, from the value of the `class` attribute—in this case, `confidential`.

Inside the curly brackets, you can have one or more *declarations*. A declaration such as this one consists of a `property`—in this example, `font-family`, separated by a colon from its value or values:

```
font-family:Arial,sans-serif;
```

When more than one value exists in a declaration, they are separated by a comma from each other. The end of a declaration is signaled by a semicolon character.

Limitations of CSS Styling

When CSS style sheets are used in the absence of XSLT stylesheets, they have significant limitations with XML documents.

Suppose that you had an XML document with the following structure:

```
<FaultReports>
<Fault status="resolved">
Internet Explorer will not save HTML files correctly.
</Fault>
<Fault status="ongoing">
Noisy telephone line to West building. Intermittent loss of
  Internet connection.
</Fault>
<Fault status="resolved">
Modem fails to dial external numbers correctly.
</Fault>
</FaultReports>
```

For example, imagine that you wanted to sort the data so that all ongoing fault reports were grouped and were followed in the displayed document by all resolved fault reports. CSS alone doesn't enable you to carry out that restructuring of an XML document.

Suppose also that you want to display an image to illustrate something about our data. CSS cannot link images.

> **Note** Some XML application languages, such as Scalable Vector Graphics (see Chapter 15, "Presenting XML Graphically—SVG"), do have functionality to display vector and bitmap images.

Some Examples Using CSS Styling

If your XML data is structured as you want to display it, you can effectively use CSS to display XML content.

Listing 13.1 shows a CSS style sheet to display heading information in red and paragraph text in a smaller, black font.

LISTING 13.1   Reports.css: A CSS Style Sheet to Display Reports Stored in XML

```
header{font-family:Arial, sans-serif;
       font-size:18;
       color:blue;}
content{ {font-family:"Times New Roman", serif;
       font-size:12;
       color:black;}
```

The XML source document is shown in Listing 13.2.

LISTING 13.2   Reports.xml: A Brief XML Data Store of Reports

```
<?xml version='1.0'?>
<?xml-stylesheet href="Reports.css" type="text/css" ?>
<Reports>
<Report>
 <header>Some interesting report</header>
 <content>Some fascinating content.</content>
</Report>
<Report>
 <header>Another interesting report</header>
 <content>Yet more fascinating content.</content>
</Report>
</Reports>
```

The xml-stylesheet processing instruction associates the XML document with the Reports.css CSS style sheet.

Figure 13.1 shows the onscreen appearance when Listing 13.2 is displayed in the Mozilla 1.0 browser.

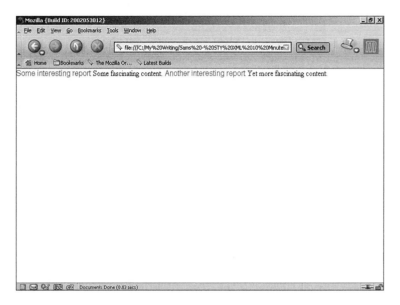

FIGURE 13.1   Basic CSS display with all element content on same line.

The display in Figure 13.1 is pretty rudimentary. It doesn't even split headings (in blue) into separate lines from the content of an individual report. That limitation in XML documents occurs because some effects seemingly produced by CSS in HTML Web pages are the result of the characteristics of the HTML elements, such as the h1 element or the p element, which automatically create a block display.

Listing 13.3 shows how you can modify the CSS style sheet, using the display property, to display the content of each element on a separate line.

LISTING 13.3   Reports2.css: Adding Block Display to the CSS Style Sheet

```
header{font-family:Arial, sans-serif;
       font-size:18;
       color:blue;
       display:block;}
```

LISTING 13.3 Continued

```
content{ {font-family:"Times New Roman", serif;
        font-size:12;
        color:black;
        display:block;}}
```

After the XML file has been amended to point to the revised CSS file, the onscreen appearance in the Mozilla browser should look like Figure 13.2. The altered XML document, Reports2.xml, is available in the code download.

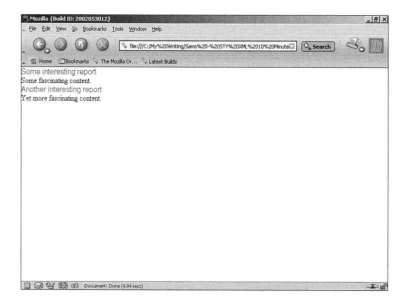

FIGURE 13.2   Appearance after the CSS has been modified to specify block display.

If you want to target only browsers that fully support CSS2, you can use absolute positioning to further refine the appearance onscreen. But, in practice, you will run into a problem when you want to reorder elements or display certain elements only. Of course, you can begin to modify the source XML document and add `class` attributes to enable you to hide a class by specifying `display:none` in a rule. However, taking that approach is ill advised. You are beginning to modify the structure of your content to control presentation, which is where HTML caused difficulties. It's an approach that runs against the principles that XML was designed to follow.

Rather than stretching CSS and modifying XML documents to accommodate CSS's limitations, it makes more sense, at least for the moment, to use CSS in conjunction with XSLT.

Using CSS with XSLT

If CSS (at least at Level 2) can't do all that you want with your XML data, you need to explore alternative approaches to displaying that data for some uses. One productive possibility is to use CSS and XSLT together with a source XML data store.

Using XSLT and CSS with HTML Output

If you use both XSLT to create HTML output documents (Web pages) and CSS styling together with the HTML, all four ways of using CSS to style HTML documents are, in principle, available:

- Linking to an external CSS style sheet using the `link` element
- Using the `@import` directive
- Using the `style` element
- Styling individual HTML elements

One of the reasons for using CSS is that it makes it easier to update styles site-wide, so you most likely will want to use an external CSS style sheet. An external CSS style sheet can be accessed using the `link` element or the `@import` directive. The `link` element is used in the example that follows.

Suppose that you wanted to use the CSS style sheet shown in Listing 13.4 site-wide in an HTML site whose pages are generated using XSLT.

LISTING 13.4   MySite.css: A Brief CSS Style Sheet

```
/* This style sheet is to be used site-wide with HTML pages
   generated using XSLT */
h1 {font-family:Arial, sans-serif;
    font-size:28;
    color:#FF0000;}

h2 {font-family:Arial, sans-serif;
    font-size:20;
    color:#0000FF;}

p {font-family:"Times New Roman", serif;
   font-size:16;
   color:black;}

li {font-family:"Times New Roman", serif;
    font-size:14;
    color:#999999;}
```

The source XML document is shown in Listing 13.5.

LISTING 13.5   CSSInformation.xml: A Brief Data Store of Information About CSS

```
<?xml version='1.0'?>
<CSSInformation>
<Techniques>
<Technique>
The &lt;link&gt; element
</Technique>
<Technique>
The @import directive
</Technique>
<Technique>
The &lt;style&gt; element
</Technique>
<Technique>
Styling individual elements
</Technique>
</Techniques>
</CSSInformation>
```

Listing 13.6 is an XSLT stylesheet to create the desired HTML output document.

LISTING 13.6   CSSInformation.xsl: An XSLT Stylesheet
Creating a Link to a CSS Style Sheet

```xml
<?xml version='1.0'?>
<xsl:stylesheet
 version="1.0"
 xmlns:xsl="http://www.w3.org/1999/XSL/Transform"
 >
<xsl:output method="html"
 indent="yes" />
<xsl:template match="/">
<html>
<head>
<title>Techniques for using CSS in HTML</title>
<link rel="stylesheet" href="MySite.css" />
</head>
<body>
<h1>Techniques for using CSS in HTML</h1>
<h2>Techniques</h2>
<p>The following are the techniques available in CSS2 to use
 CSS.</p>
<ul>
<xsl:apply-templates select="//Technique" />
</ul>
</body>
</html>
</xsl:template>

<xsl:template match="Technique">
<li><xsl:value-of select="."/></li>
</xsl:template>

</xsl:stylesheet>
```

Notice the link element in the head section of the literal result elements
in the XSLT stylesheet. The rel and href attributes of the link element
indicate that the file MySite.css (see Listing 13.4) is to be linked as the
CSS style sheet for the HTML document.

Listing 13.7 shows the HTML output document.

LISTING 13.7   CSSInformation.html: The Result of the XSLT Transformation

```html
<html>
 <head>
  <meta http-equiv="Content-Type" content="text/html;
    charset=utf-8">
  <title>Techniques for using CSS in HTML</title>
  <link rel="stylesheet" href="MySite.css">
 </head>
 <body>
  <h1>Techniques for using CSS in HTML</h1>
  <h2>Techniques</h2>
  <p>The following are the techniques available in CSS2
    to use CSS.</p>
  <ul>
   <li>
    The &lt;link&gt; element
   </li>
   <li>
    The @import directive
   </li>
   <li>
    The &lt;style&gt; element
   </li>
   <li>
    Styling individual elements
   </li>
  </ul>
 </body>
</html>
```

Figure 13.3 shows the onscreen appearance. When you view the document onscreen, you can see by the size, font family, and color of the text that the CSS styling in MySite.css has been applied to the text in the HTML page.

Combining CSS with XSLT in this way maintains the separation of content and presentation in XML documents. At the same time, linking external CSS style sheets offers the maintenance benefits of CSS.

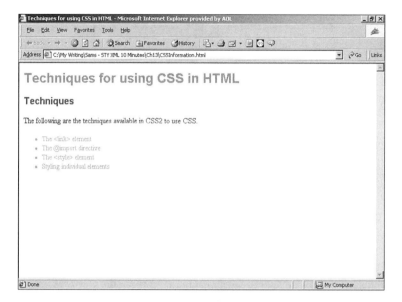

FIGURE 13.3   An HTML document displayed using CSS but created using an XSLT transformation.

Summary

This lesson discussed the need for Cascading Style Sheets (CSS) to ease maintenance of Web sites. It also described and demonstrated the way to link an XML document to an external CSS style. In addition, you learned about the styling of XML documents and the advantages of using CSS together with XSLT, for example, when elements need to be reordered.

LESSON 14
Linking in XML—XLink

In this lesson, you will learn how to use the XML Linking Language (XLink) simple links and the XML Pointer Language (XPointer).

The XML Linking Language

The XML Linking Language (XLink)—and the associated XML Pointer Language (XPointer) specification, discussed later in this chapter—are intended to provide linking functionality for XML on the Web. This will provide XML-based linking functionality equivalent to HTML, but with significant enhancements. Relevant parts of XLink and XPointer have already been implemented in Scalable Vector Graphics (see Chapter 15, "Presenting XML Graphically—SVG") and likely will be implemented in at least some other XML specifications.

The original vision for XML was that it should be used on the Web. However, in practice it has displaced HTML much more slowly than was originally envisioned. Perhaps a contributing factor to that was the lengthy delay in finishing development of the XLink and the (still unfinished) XPointer specifications.

XLink became a full W3C Recommendation in June 2001 (see www.w3.org/TR/2001/REC-xlink-20010627/). At the time of this writing, four new XPointer Working Drafts have just been issued.

XLink provides *simple links*, which are similar to HTML hyperlinks, and *extended links* that introduce functionality beyond that provided in HTML. XPointer is a much more powerful fragment-identifier mechanism than HTML anchors.

First let's look at HTML hyperlinks and their strengths and limitations. XPointer is discussed later in the chapter.

XLink and HTML Hyperlinks

HTML hyperlinking has been immensely successful as a pivotal part of the World Wide Web. The Web is almost unimaginable without such hyperlinking functionality.

In HTML, the hyperlinking mechanism uses the a element. It is possible to use the a element to link externally to other HTML Web pages or other resources, or to link internally or externally to specified document fragments.

These simple mechanisms are immensely useful, but they do have limitations. For example, a link is expressed at one end only. If you click a link on page A and move to page B, the browser Back button typically allows you to link back to page A. But if you visit page B directly, there is likely no way to link to page A at all.

To take another example, if you want to link to a fragment of page B but the document author hasn't provided an anchor at the point that interests you, you can't link directly to that point. You are limited to linking to the Web page and providing instructions for what part of the document you want a user to scroll to.

XLink and XPointer were intended to address limitations such as these.

Simple Links and Extended Links

XLink provides two significantly different types of links: *simple links* and *extended links*.

An XLink simple link behaves on its own very much like an HTML hyperlink. When used with XPointer, it is potentially much more flexible in linking to specified document fragments.

XLink extended links allow links to be created among more than two resources.

XLink Jargon

XLink brings with it a lot of jargon, which is needed to precisely express what is happening with XLink extended links.

In XLink terminology, a *link* is simply an explicit association between two or more resources. The link is made explicit by an XLink *linking element*.

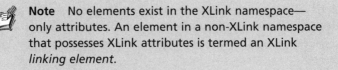

Note No elements exist in the XLink namespace—only attributes. An element in a non-XLink namespace that possesses XLink attributes is termed an XLink *linking element*.

So, an XLink simple link might look like this:

```
<myPrefix:myElement xlink:href="SomeResource.xml" ... />
```

The preceding code assumes that the XLink namespace URI, www.w3.org/1999/xlink, has been declared at an appropriate place in the document.

Using or following an XLink link is termed *traversal*. The resource that contains the XLink linking element is known as the *starting resource*, and the destination of the link is the *ending resource*.

A *local resource* is an XML element that participates in a link by virtue of having a linking element as its parent or being itself a linking element. A *remote resource* is addressed by means of a URI reference.

A link that has a *local starting resource* and a *remote ending resource* is termed *outbound*. XLink simple links, like HTML hyperlinks, are of this type.

XLink also allows two other types of arc: *inbound* and *third-party*. An inbound arc exists when the XLink linking element is expressed on a local resource—in other words, there is a local ending resource and a remote starting resource. A third-party link exists when the XLink linking element is expressed in neither the starting resource nor the ending resource. These types of links, which are XLink extended links, can be used to form link databases, also called *linkbases*.

XLink Attributes

The XLink specification creates no new elements but does add attributes that are in the XLink namespace to elements in other XML application languages. Typically, the XLink namespace must be declared.

The xlink:href attribute specifies a URI for the remote resource. The type of an XLink—simple or extended—is expressed using the xlink:type attribute. For a simple link that replaces the local resource when the arc is traversed, you need only those two attributes:

```
<myPrefix:myElement xlink:type="simple"
xlink:href="someURI" >
```

The xlink:show attribute controls where the remote resource is displayed. The default value is replace. To display a resource in a new browser window, the xlink:show attribute has the value new.

The xlink:actuate attribute controls when the arc of the link is traversed. The default value is onRequest. To traverse an arc upon document loading, the xlink:actuate attribute has the value onLoad. At the time of this writing, no browser implements that feature.

An extended link has the xlink:type attribute with the value extended. An extended link may have xlink:href, xlink:show, and xlink:actuate attributes. In addition, it may have xlink:title, xlink:resource, xlink:arc, xlink:arcrole, xlink:label, xlink:from, and xlink:to attributes. The latter attributes will not be discussed further.

XLink Examples

At the time of this writing, Internet Explorer browser has no support for XLink. The Netscape 6.*x* and Mozilla 1.*x* browsers support XLink simple links only.

Listings 14.1 and 14.2 show two brief XML documents that each contain a single XLink simple link.

LISTING 14.1   Document1.xml: A Document with a Single
XLink Simple Link

```
<?xml version='1.0'?>
<?xml-stylesheet href="BigText.css" type="text/css" ?>
<Document1 xmlns:xlink="http://www.w3.org/1999/xlink">
<myPrefix:myElement xlink:href="Document2.xml"
 xlink:type="simple"
 xmlns:myPrefix="http://www.XMML.com/">
Click here to go to Document 2.
</myPrefix:myElement>
</Document1>
```

LISTING 14.2   Document2.xml: A Document with Another
Simple Link

```
<?xml version='1.0'?>
<?xml-stylesheet href="BigText.css" type="text/css" ?>
<Document1 xmlns:xlink="http://www.w3.org/1999/xlink">
<myPrefix:myElement xlink:href="Document1.xml"
 xlink:type="simple"
 xmlns:myPrefix="http://www.XMML.com/">
Click here to go back to Document 1.
</myPrefix:myElement>
</Document1>
```

Notice that the XLink namespace is declared in each listing on the document element. For ease of display in the screenshots, the documents have been linked to a CSS style sheet shown in Listing 14.3.

LISTING 14.3   BigText.css: A CSS Style Sheet Controlling the
Appearance of Text

```
myElement {
font-family:Arial, sans-serif;
font-size:30pt;
color:blue;
text-decoration:underline;
}
```

Without the CSS stylesheet, the XML text would be displayed as black, without underlining, and in the default font.

Figure 14.1 shows Listing 14.1 displayed in the Mozilla 1.0 browser. Note that the cursor changes to a pointing finger cursor over the linking text.

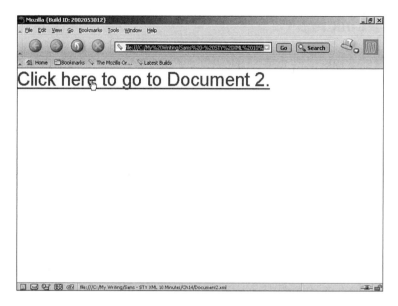

FIGURE 14.1   Linking text in a simple XML document in the Mozilla browser.

If you wanted Listing 14.2 to display in a new browser window, you could simply add an `xlink:show` attribute with the value of `new`, as shown in Listing 14.4.

LISTING 14.4   Document3.xml: A Link to Open a New Browser Window

```
<?xml version='1.0'?>
<?xml-stylesheet href="BigText.css" type="text/css" ?>
<Document1 xmlns:xlink="http://www.w3.org/1999/xlink">
<myPrefix:myElement xlink:href="Document2.xml"
 xlink:type="simple"
 xlink:show="new"
 xmlns:myPrefix="http://www.XMML.com/">
Click here to go to Document 2.
</myPrefix:myElement>
</Document1>
```

XLink in SVG

One of the XML application languages that already implements XLink simple links is the W3C's Scalable Vector Graphics (SVG) specification. SVG 1.0 does not support XLink extended links. An XLink example in SVG is shown in Chapter 15.

Having looked at how you can link whole Web pages, let's move on to see how XPointer handles XML fragment identifiers.

Document Fragments and XPointer

In HTML documents, the process of addressing a specific part of the document involves using anchors. This can be a useful mechanism, but it does have significant limitations.

 Caution Immediately before this writing, the XPointer specification was split into four W3C Working Drafts. The description that follows is based on those drafts and, therefore, is potentially subject to change.

Let's suppose that you want to link to the HTML document shown in Listing 14.5. It includes many br tags to space out the anchors.

LISTING 14.5   Anchors.html: An HTML Document with Anchors

```
<!DOCTYPE HTML PUBLIC "-//W3C//DTD HTML 4.0 Transitional//EN"
"http://www.w3.org/TR/REC-html40/loose.dtd">
<HTML>
<HEAD>
<TITLE>Teach Yourself XML in 10 Minutes - Chapter 14</TITLE>
</HEAD>
<BODY>
<h1>
Linking in XML - XLink
</h1>
<a name="Anchor1">
```

LISTING 14.5 Continued

```
<p>First fascinating text.</p>
</a>
<br /><br /><br /><br /><br />
<a name="Anchor2">
<p>Second fascinating text.</p>
</a>
<br /><br /><br /><br /><br />
<a name="Anchor3">
<p>Third fascinating text.</p>
</a>
<br /><br /><br /><br /><br />
<br /><br /><br /><br /><br />
<br /><br /><br /><br /><br />
<p>The REALLY fascinating text.</p>
<br /><br /><br /><br /><br />
<br /><br /><br /><br /><br />
</BODY>
</HTML>
```

If you want to link from another HTML document to any of the specified anchors in Listing 14.5, writing a link is straightforward:

```
<a href="Anchors.html#anchorName" ...> LinkText</a>
```

If you don't have write privileges on the target document, you have limited options. You can ask the Web page author to add an anchor at the point that you want to link to (often unrealistic in a rapidly growing Web), link to an anchor close to the real point of interest (if there is such an anchor), or accept that it isn't possible to link to a desired fragment in that page.

XPointer is designed to provide improved functionality for linking to document fragments in XML documents. A correctly written XPointer should be capable of identifying any arbitrary part of an XML document. How that part of the document is processed after it is identified depends on the application with which the XPointer processor is associated.

For example, suppose you wanted to link to a long XML document, perhaps a lengthy report, and display it in a browser or similar software at exactly the point of interest. You could write an XPointer to access any part of the document that is of interest without having write access to the target document.

> **Note**   At the time of this writing, no XPointer tools conform fully to the newly issued XPointer draft documents.

To understand how to do that, you should look first at the relationship between XPath (discussed in Chapter 9, "The XML Path Language— XPath"), and XPointer.

XPointer and XPath

XPath models an XML document as a hierarchy of nodes. XPointer incorporates the concept of a node and also makes use of XPath functions, some of which were discussed in Chapter 9.

The XPath notion of a node is generalized in XPointer to include the additional notions of a *point* and a *range*. The following XML code snippet can help illustrate these concepts.

```
<text>Here is some text.</text>
```

All the text between the start and end tags of the text element is the value of a corresponding text node. The point exactly between the initial H and the first e of Here is a point. That type of point is a *character-point*.

A range could be the text string is some, with the *starting point* between the space character and the initial i of is, and the *ending point* between the final e of some and the following space character.

XPath operates using location paths. The output from one location step is used as the input for the following location step. XPointer works similarly. The *location set* returned by one pointer part is the start for processing by the next pointer part, if there is one.

XPointer incorporates XPath functions and adds functions that manipulate or return points and ranges.

Node tests in XPath have a counterpart—a *test*—in XPointer. An XPointer test can be applied to a node, point, or range.

The XPointer Framework and Schemes

As this book was being written, a significant rewrite of the XPointer specification emerged after (from a public viewpoint) a static period of several months. The XPointer draft specification was split into four documents: the XPointer Framework Working Draft and three draft specifications that describe XPointer *schemes*—the xpointer(), xmlns(), and element() schemes.

An XPointer processor takes as input an XML document and a URI that includes a fragment identifier. The output from an XPointer processor is either identification of a part of the XML document corresponding to the fragment identifier or an error.

The XPointer Framework

The XPointer Framework is a specification that defines the context for the xpointer(), xmlns(), and element() schemes.

Scheme-Based XPointers

A scheme-based XPointer consists of one or more *pointer parts*, each of which is of the following general form:

```
schemeName(characterSequence)+
```

In other words, the *pointer part* begins with the scheme name followed by an opening parenthesis. A sequence of XML characters follows, and the pointer part is completed by a closing parenthesis.

So, an XPointer from the xpointer() scheme to select Chapter element nodes would look like this:

```
xpointer(//Chapter)
```

If the sequence of XML characters contains an unbalanced parenthesis character, that unbalanced parenthesis must be escaped.

As indicated by the + cardinality operator, an XPointer may use more than one scheme.

You will look at each of the proposed XPointer schemes in turn. First, let's look at the xpointer() scheme.

The xpointer() Scheme

The xpointer() scheme is the most extensive of the XPointer schemes. In fact, it was originally envisaged as being the only scheme until technical issues led to the development of the xmlns() scheme (discussed later in this chapter).

The xpointer() scheme is associated with the namespace URI www.w3.org/2001/05/XPointer.

Caution   The namespace URI given is associated with a Working Draft for the xpointer() scheme. It is possible that the namespace URI will change for the final version of the specification.

Points in the xpointer() Scheme

The xpointer() scheme recognizes two types of points: a *node-point* and a *character-point*. Both types of points are defined in terms of a container node (the node within whose content the point is situated) and an index.

A node-point is a point between nodes that are children of the *container node* of the point. The index for a node-point lies between zero (the index of the node-point immediately before the first node in the container node) and the number of child nodes that the container node has.

A node-point corresponds conceptually to a gap between nodes. Because character-points occur within nodes, they are envisaged as occurring between the node-points before and after their container node.

The self axis and the descendant-or-self axis of a point location contain the point itself. The parent axis contains the container node of the point. The ancestor axis contains the container node and its ancestors. The ancestor-or-self axis also contains the point itself. All other axes are empty.

Points do not have an expanded name, and the string value of a point is the empty string.

Ranges in the `xpointer()` Scheme

A range is defined by its *start point* and its *end point*. A range consists of all the XML structure and content between the start point and the end point of the range. The start point of a range need not be in the same node as the end point if the container node of the start point is of type root, element, or text. However, both points must be in the same XML document or external parsed entity. The start point must not come later in the document than the end point.

A special case arises when the start point and the end point are the same point. In that case, the range is referred to as a *collapsed range*.

A range does not have an expanded name. The string value of a range consists of the character content of text nodes inside the range.

The axes of a range are identical to the axes of its start point. The parent axis of the range contains the parent node of the start point.

The XPointer `start-point()` and `end-point()` functions can be used to navigate to the start point and end point, respectively, of a range.

Functions in the `xpointer()` Scheme

The `xpointer()` scheme adds functions to those available from the XPath function library.

The `string-range()` function takes two required arguments (a location set and a string) and two optional arguments (numbers). The `string-range()` function returns a location for each occurrence of the string argument in the location set argument.

The `range()` function takes a location set argument and returns a location set. The `range()` function returns a covering range for each location in the argument location set.

> **Note** A *covering range* is a range that totally encom-
> passes a location. For a range, the covering range is
> the same range. For a point, the start point and end
> point of the covering range are the point itself.
> Definitions of other covering ranges are included in
> the XPointer specification.

The `range-inside()` function returns a location set and takes a single
location set argument.

The `range-to()` function returns a range for each location in the context
whose start point is returned by the `start-point()` function and whose
end point is returned by the `end-point()` function.

The `start-point()` and `end-point()` functions respectively address the
starting point and ending point of a range.

The `here()` function is meaningful only when the context is an XML document or an external parsed entity. If the expression being evaluated is in
a text node inside an element node, the `here()` function returns the element node. Otherwise the `here()` function returns the node that directly
contains the expression being evaluated.

The `origin()` function is meaningful only when it is processed in
response to traversal of a link expressed in an XML document.

Some `xpointer()` Scheme Examples

To locate an element node that has an ID attribute of value `"CRES99"`, you
can write this:

```
xpointer(id("CRES99"))
```

If you want to reference a range that includes the first and second chapters
of a document, you could write this:

```
xpointer(//chapter[number='1'])/range-to(//chapter[number='2'])
```

This assumes that the document contains `chapter` elements with a `number`
attribute corresponding to the chapter number.

The xmlns() Scheme

The xmlns() scheme is intended for use with the XPointer Framework to ensure correct interpretation of namespace prefixes in XPointers.

You might assume that using namespace prefixes would be possible using only the xpointer() scheme, but take a look at the following XML code snippet and think of the ambiguity it introduces:

```
<myPrefix:myElement
 xmlns:myPrefix="http://www.XMML.com/Namespace">
 <AnElement>
 First piece of text.
 </AnElement>
 <myPrefix:myElement
 xmlns:myPrefix="http://www.XMML.com/AnotherNamespace">
 <AnElement>
 Second piece of text.
 </AnElement>
 <!-- Some content could go here -->
 </myPrefix:myElement>
</myPrefix:myElement>
```

If you had the XPointer that follows, which XPointer location(s) is it intended to refer to?

```
xpointer(//myPrefix:myElement/AnElement)
```

Is it intended to refer to both AnElement elements? Or only one? If so, which? The myPrefix:myElement is declared to be associated with two different namespaces. For an XML processor, that doesn't cause difficulties because it uses the namespace URI, not the namespace prefix. But for XPointer you need to specify which namespace URI you are referring to.

To remove that ambiguity, the xmlns() scheme has been provided.

You can refer unambiguously to the outer myPrefix:myElement element using the following XPointer:

```
xmlns(myPrefix:http://www.XMML.com/Namespace)
 xpointer(//myPrefix:myElement/AnElement)
```

Or, you can refer unambiguously to the inner one using this:

```
xmlns(myPrefix:http://www.XMML.com/AnotherNamespace)
 xpointer(//myPrefix:myElement/AnElement)
```

Remember that an XML processor uses the expanded name rather than the namespace prefix for processing. So, if you want to access both `AnElement` elements, you could use both `xmlns()` pointer parts:

```
xmlns(a:http://www.XMML.com/Namespace)
   xmlns(b:http://www.XMML.com/AnotherNamespace)
```

You could use `a` or `b` as the namespace prefix in further pointer parts using the `xpointer()` scheme.

The `element()` Scheme

The `element()` scheme is intended to be used with the XPointer Framework to provide basic addressing of elements in XML documents.

The `element()` scheme can use two forms of syntax: a name or a child sequence.

Suppose you had the following XML document:

```
<myDocument>
<Introduction>Some text</Introduction>
<MainText>Some main text</MainText>
<Postscript>Some postscript text</Postscript>
</myDocument>
```

You could select the `MainText` element by name using this line:

```
element(//MainText)
```

Or, you could select it as a child sequence using this code:

```
element(/1/2)
```

The syntax of the child sequence is to be understood as follows. The initial / character indicates that the root node is the initial context location. The `1` indicates that you are selecting the first element child of the root node—in this case, the `myDocument` element node. The next / character is a separator. The `2` indicates that you are selecting the second element child node of the `myDocument` node—in this case, the `MainText` element node.

Summary

In this lesson, you were introduced to the XML Linking Language and learned how to use XLink simple links. The chapter also described the XML Pointer Language and introduced the characteristics of the XPointer Framework and the `xpointer()`, `xmlns()`, and `element()` schemes.

LESSON 15

Presenting XML Graphically— SVG

In this lesson, you will be introduced to Scalable Vector Graphics (SVG), an XML application language that expresses two-dimensional vector graphics.

What Is SVG?

SVG is an XML application language that is intended to replace many uses of bitmap graphics on the Web and provide a vector graphics standard that is not vendor-specific (compare Microsoft's VML) and that is open source (compare Macromedia's Flash/SWF). SVG is written in XML-compliant syntax.

Version 1.0 of SVG became a W3C Recommendation in September 2001. At the time of this writing, version 1.1 of SVG is a W3C Candidate Recommendation (www.w3.org/TR/SVG11/) and will provide modularization of SVG so that SVG can be used on mobile browsers as well as on traditional desktop browsers.

SVG code is always well-formed SVG and can be validated against a publicly available DTD. SVG has elements for displaying text—text and tspan—as well as several elements that represent commonly used graphics shapes—for example, rect, circle, ellipse, and polygon. A path element can be used to represent any arbitrary two-dimensional graphics shape.

An SVG shape has its onscreen position, its dimensions, and its style information specified by attributes. The following code specifies a circle shape of radius 50 pixels filled with green and having a red outline (*stroke* in SVG jargon):

```
<circle cx="100px" cy="100px" r="50px"
style="fill:#00FF00; stroke:#FF0000; stroke-width:3" />
```

Alternatively, styling information for an SVG image or Web page can be contained in an internal style sheet (contained in a `style` element) or in an external CSS style sheet, referenced using the `xml-stylesheet` processing instruction. An internal style sheet contains non-XML text, so it must be contained in a `CDATA` section:

```
<style type="text/css">
<![CDATA[
/* style rules go here. */
]]>
</style>
```

In addition to static shapes and text, SVG provides five animation elements—`set`, `animate`, `animateMotion`, `animateColor`, and `animateTransform`—that singly or combined can produce an essentially unlimited number of animation effects.

SVG code is XML, so data stored as generic XML can be transformed into SVG using an XSLT stylesheet. This allows SVG charts to be created to express bar charts, line charts, and so on. Another growing use of SVG is to express map data.

In addition to containing SVG elements that define graphics shapes and text, SVG can be used to display external vector or bitmap images. For example, the following SVG code could be used to display a PNG image called myBitmap.png:

```
<image xlink:href="myBitmap.png" x="240px" y="90px"
width="350px" height="125px" />
```

In addition, SVG enables the scripting of a Document Object Model (DOM), which incorporates the DOM Level 2 (to be discussed in Chapter 16, "The Document Object Model," and Chapter 17, "The Document

Object Model—2). Script code may be contained in a script element, as shown here:

```
<script type="text/javascript" >
[![CDATA[
// JavaScript code is not XML and needs to be in a
// CDATA section.
]]>
</script>
```

Or, it may be referenced in an external JavaScript or ECMAScript file:

```
<script type="text/javascript" xlink:href="myJavaScript.js" />
```

SVG also includes several powerful bitmap filters that, to take a simple example, can add a drop shadow to SVG text or shapes.

Advantages of SVG

If you were around in the early days of the Web, you might remember the excitement as newcomers to HTML were able to learn the new technology rapidly because the HTML source code was always accessible in a Web browser. SVG offers the same advantage: A student of SVG can study the source code of an interesting or impressive graphic and need not deal with a steep learning curve.

The Adobe SVG Viewer can be downloaded from www.adobe.com/svg/viewer/install/main.html and is a plug-in for conventional Web browsers. The SVG source code of an image displayed in the Adobe SVG Viewer is accessed by simply right-clicking the SVG image and selecting the View Source option.

The Batik standalone SVG viewer is available for download from http://xml.apache.org/batik/. Batik can also be used in Java applications to dynamically create and display SVG.

SVG can be combined with other XML application languages. New-generation browsers such as the X-Smiles browser (www.x-smiles.org) enable multiple XML languages to be combined into XML-based Web pages. For example, you could use SVG images within an XHTML Web page that also contains forms using the XML-based XForms specification.

An alternative approach is to create all-SVG Web pages, such as those you can see at www.XMML.com/.

Creating SVG

SVG is XML. In principle, it can be created by any text editor. Of course, having syntax checking for well-formedness and color highlighting is an improvement over an editor such as Windows Notepad.

Listing 15.1 shows a simple SVG document that animates some text from a position offscreen onto the screen shortly after the document loads.

LISTING 15.1   HelloVector.svg: An Animated Greeting Expressed in SVG

```
<?xml version='1.0'?>
<!DOCTYPE svg PUBLIC "-//W3C//DTD SVG 1.0//EN"
"http://www.w3.org/TR/2001/REC-SVG-20010904/DTD/svg10.dtd">
<svg>
<text x="-320" y="50" style="font-family:Arial; font-
  size:24;">
Hello Vector Graphics World!
<animate attributeName="x" from="-320" to="20"
  begin="1s" dur="3s" fill="freeze" />
</text>
</svg>
```

The XML declaration and the DOCTYPE declaration should be familiar from earlier chapters in this book. The document element is an svg element. Remember that SVG is XML, so element type names are case sensitive. The svg element must be written using lowercase characters only.

An SVG text element is used to contain the short message. One of the SVG animation elements is used to animate the text from a position just offscreen to the left onto the screen, starting one second after the document loads.

This *declarative animation* provides powerful and flexible animation facilities in SVG, which don't need to use scripting languages for many common effects. However, SVG has the flexibility to add script code to augment animation effects when it is appropriate.

Figure 15.1 shows the onscreen appearance partway through the animation of the text.

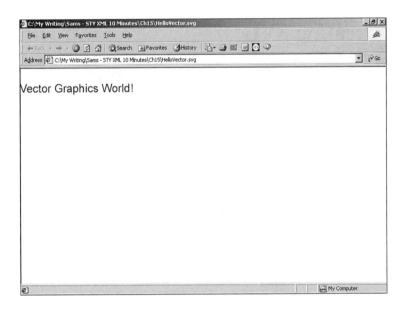

FIGURE 15.1   A simple SVG document that animates text onscreen.

To view the SVG content onscreen, you need either a Web browser that has the Adobe SVG plug-in installed (see `www.Adobe.com/svg/` for further details) or a dedicated SVG viewer such as Batik (see `http://xml.apache.org/batik/` for further information). Some of the examples in Chapters 16 and 17 use SVG to illustrate programmatic control of the XML Document Object Model, so you will find it useful to install an SVG viewer.

Examples of SVG used in geographical mapping can be seen at `www.carto.net/projects/`.

Another approach to creating SVG is to use a drawing tool with SVG export capabilities. For example, Jasc WebDraw is a dedicated SVG drawing tool. More information is available at www.Jasc.com. Other well-known vector-drawing tools such as Adobe Illustrator (version 9 and onward, www.Adobe.com) and CorelDraw (version 10 and onward, www.corel.com) have SVG export facilities. Macromedia Freehand does not support SVG export at the time of this writing.

Because SVG is XML, it can be generated dynamically from XML data stores on the server before being transmitted to an SVG-enabled Web browser. Among the server-side tools that can be used to generate SVG dynamically are XSLT, Java, and Perl.

Some SVG Examples

This section shows a few short examples of SVG code, including how to use SVG to create a rollover and how XLink is used in SVG.

SVG Rollovers

In a conventional HTML Web page, it is necessary to use JavaScript to produce rollover effects. In SVG, rollover effects can be produced using SVG declarative syntax alone. Listing 15.2 shows a simple rollover with a message about SVG.

LISTING 15.2   Mouseover.svg: A Message About SVG

```
<?xml version='1.0'?>
<!DOCTYPE svg PUBLIC "-//W3C//DTD SVG 1.0//EN"
"http://www.w3.org/TR/2001/REC-SVG-20010904/DTD/svg10.dtd">
<svg>
<rect id="myRect" x="20" y="30" rx="10"
  ry="10" width="250" height="50"
  style="fill:white; stroke:blue; stroke-width:4">
<set attributeName="fill" from="white" to="#FFFF00"
  begin="mouseover" end="mouseout" />
</rect>
<text x="35" y="65"
  style="fill:blue; stroke:none; font-family:Arial,sans-serif;
  font-size:28; pointer-events:none " visibility="visible">
```

LISTING 15.2   Continued

```
<animate begin="myRect.mouseover"
  attributeName="visibility" from="visible"
to="hidden" dur="0.1s" fill="freeze" />
<animate begin="myRect.mouseout"
  attributeName="visibility" from="hidden"
to="visible" dur="0.1s" fill="freeze" />
SVG is cool!
</text>
<text x="35" y="65"
  style="fill:red; stroke:none; font-family:Arial,sans-serif;
  font-size:28; pointer-events:none; visibility:hidden;">
<animate begin="myRect.mouseover"
  attributeName="visibility" from="hidden"
to="visible" dur="0.1s" fill="freeze" />
<animate begin="myRect.mouseout"
  attributeName="visibility" from="visible"
to="hidden" dur="0.1s" fill="freeze" />
SVG is RED HOT!
</text>
</svg>
```

When the document loads a simple text message, SVG is Cool! is visible against a white background inside a rectangle. When the rectangle is rolled over, its fill color changes to yellow, the first text message is hidden, and the message SVG is RED HOT! is displayed. The change in text is achieved by animating the visibility property of the two text elements in the document.

Figure 15.2 shows a composite image that includes both the rolled-over and unrolled-over versions of the rectangle.

XLink Links in SVG

SVG uses XLink linking mechanisms to link to external resources and uses a subset of XPointer to address fragments in the same SVG document.

Listing 15.3 shows an example of using XLink in an SVG document.

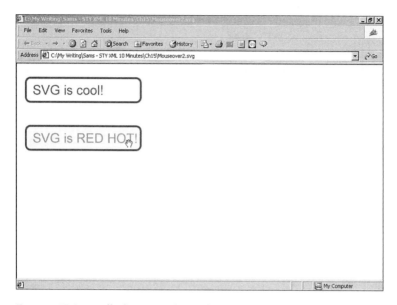

FIGURE 15.2   Rolled-over and unrolled-over versions of the rectangle.

LISTING 15.3   SVGLink.svg: An Example of Using an XLink Link in SVG

```
<?xml version='1.0'?>
<!DOCTYPE svg PUBLIC "-//W3C//DTD SVG 1.0//EN"
"http://www.w3.org/TR/2001/REC-SVG-20010904/DTD/svg10.dtd">
<svg>
<rect x="0" y="0" width="100%" height="100%"
  style="fill:#FFFFFF" />
<a xlink:href="http://www.XMML.com/" >
<text x="20" y="30"
  style="fill:#666666; stroke:none; font-family:
  'Times New Roman', serif; font-size:24" >
Link to the XMML.com all-SVG Web site.
</text>
</a>
</svg>
```

The SVG a element uses an `xlink:href` attribute to specify the resource to be traversed to. As you can see in Figure 15.3, rolling over the text causes a pointing-finger cursor to appear. Clicking the text links to the www.XMML.com all-SVG Web site.

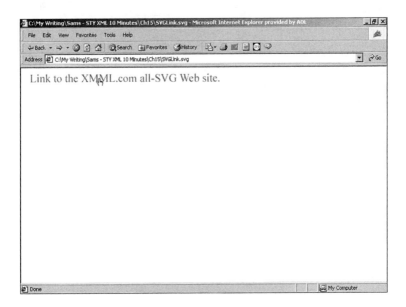

FIGURE 15.3   An XLink hyperlink to an external resource.

Using XPointer to Reference Definitions

SVG documents, other than very short ones, likely will include a definitions section contained in a defs element.

Listing 15.4 shows an example of using a *bare names* XPointer (now called *shorthand form* in the XPointer drafts that came out after the SVG 1.0 Recommendation was completed) to reference the definition of an SVG filter that applies a drop shadow to the text.

LISTING 15.4   Reference.svg: Applying an SVG Filter on Mouseover

```
<?xml version='1.0'?>
<!DOCTYPE svg PUBLIC "-//W3C//DTD SVG 1.0//EN"
"http://www.w3.org/TR/2001/REC-SVG-20010904/DTD/svg10.dtd">
<svg>
```

LISTING 15.4   Continued

```
<defs>
<style type="text/css">
<![CDATA[
text {font-family:Arial, sans-serif;
font-size:16;
fill:black;
stroke:none;
}
text.big {font-family:Arial, sans-serif;
font-size:35;
fill:black;
stroke:none;
}
]]>
</style>
<filter id="myFilter" width="140%" height="140%" y="-20%">
<feGaussianBlur in="SourceAlpha" stdDeviation="2.5"
   result="Blur" />
<feOffset in="Blur" dx="3" dy="3" result="OffsetBlur" />
<feMerge>
<feMergeNode in="OffsetBlur" />
<feMergeNode in="SourceGraphic" />
</feMerge>
</filter>
</defs>
<text x="20" y="20" >
Mouse the text below and watch a drop shadow being applied to
   it.
</text>
<text class="big" x="20" y="120" filter="none">
<set begin="mouseover" end="mouseout"
   attributeName="fill" from="black" to="red" />
<set begin="mouseover" end="mouseout"
   attributeName="filter" from="none" to="url(#myFilter)" />
Sams Teach Yourself XML in 10 Minutes
</text>
<text class="big" x="20" y="220" filter="none">
<set begin="mouseover" end="mouseout"
   attributeName="fill" from="black" to="red" />
<set begin="mouseover" end="mouseout"
   attributeName="filter" from="none" to="url(#myFilter)" />
Sams Teach Yourself XML in 10 Minutes
</text>
</svg>
```

Figure 15.4 is a composite image with both rolled-over and unrolled-over text.

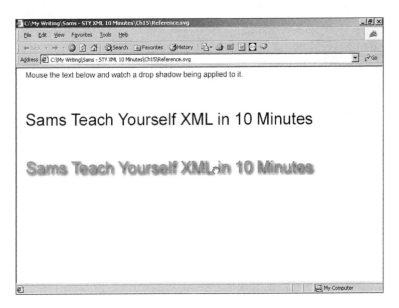

FIGURE 15.4   A drop shadow created using SVG filter elements in response to rolling over the text

This short chapter has been able to indicate only a few of SVG's capabilities. Appendix B, "XML Tools," gives some information about Web sites and mailing lists where you can explore SVG further.

Summary

This lesson introduced the reasons for the development of SVG and explained some of its advantages. It also described and demonstrated a number of SVG 1.0 elements, the use of XLink in SVG and an example of using an SVG filter.

LESSON 16
The Document Object Model

In this lesson, you will learn the basics of how to program the XML Document Object Model.

The Document Object Model

The Document Object Model (DOM) is a series of W3C specifications that provide increasing functionality to access and manipulate XML (and HTML) documents programmatically. The DOM provides a practical way to manipulate, create, and modify XML documents programmatically.

At the time of this writing, the DOM Level 2 specifications (see Appendix B, "XML Tools," for links) are the current versions. DOM Level 3 specifications are in development.

> **Note** Only the DOM Level 2 Core interfaces are considered in this chapter and in Chapter 17, "The Document Object Model—2." The Document Object Model Level 2 also specifies more specialized interfaces to be used—for example, with HTML documents and CSS style sheets.

Object and Interfaces

The name of the Document Object Model refers to *objects*, but the DOM is defined in terms of *interfaces*. An object packages a specified group of *properties* and *methods* in a convenient object, for want of a better term.

A property can be thought of as a characteristic of an object. For example, a car might have a `color` property and a `number_of_wheels` property. Each of these properties tells about some characteristic of the car. Similarly, a `car` object might have `go_forward()`, `go_backwards()`, and `stop()` methods. These methods would tell something about what the object can do.

An interface can be thought of as a convenient package of properties and methods. An object can implement an interface—a specified and named package of properties and methods. It can either add properties and methods specific to that object or can implement the properties and methods defined in one or more other interfaces.

You learned earlier that an XML document can be viewed as a logical hierarchy. In the DOM, you can model that hierarchy using several nodes.

Let's look at a simple XML document and consider how it is represented in the DOM. Figure 16.1 shows a hierarchy representing the interfaces and objects that make up the DOM representation of the document.

```
<book edition="1">
Sams Teach Yourself XML in 10 Minutes
</book>
```

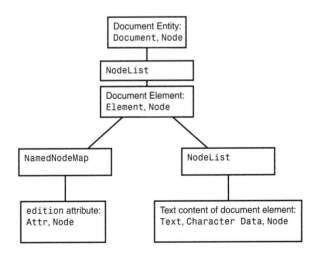

FIGURE 16.1 A hierarchical representation of the example document.

Let's first look at Figure 16.1 and consider each part of the hierarchy. Later you will look at individual interfaces shown in the figure in more detail.

The node at the apex of the hierarchy represents the (invisible) document entity of an XML document. That node implements the Document interface and the Node interface.

The next node in the hierarchy implements the NodeList interface. In this simple document there is only a single node that is the child of the NodeList—the node representing the document element, the book element, of the XML document. That node implements the Node interface and the Element interface.

The Element node has a child node that implements the NamedNodeList interface as its child node. That node has a single child node that represents the edition attribute in the XML document. The node implements the Attr and Node interfaces.

That Element node also has a node that implements the NodeList interface as a child node. In this simple document, there is only a single node that contains the text content of the Book element node. That node implements the Node, Text, and CharacterData interfaces.

DOM Interfaces

Let's examine in more detail the interfaces in Figure 16.1.

The Node Interface

As you saw in Figure 16.1, many DOM nodes implement the Node interface. They might also have other properties and methods in addition to those that the Node interface provides.

These DOM interfaces are said to *extend* the Node interface. Figure 16.2 shows the interfaces in DOM Level 2 Core that extend the Node interface.

In general, the names of the node types that inherit from the Node interface can be readily understood from their names. The DocumentType interface, for example, corresponds to the DOCTYPE declaration.

DOM interfaces can be extended several levels deep. Figure 16.3 shows the node types that extend the CharacterData interface.

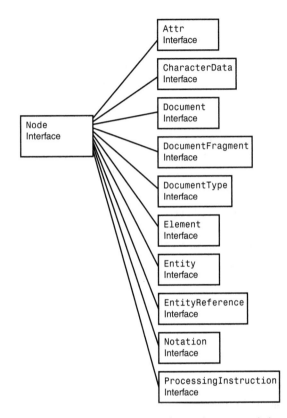

FIGURE 16.2   The DOM Level 2 interfaces that extend the Node interface.

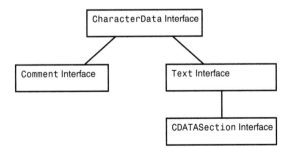

FIGURE 16.3   The interfaces that extend the CharacterData interface.

Both the Comment and Text interfaces extend the CharacterData interface. The Text interface itself is extended by the CDATASection interface. You will look at these text-oriented interfaces later, but first let's look briefly at the properties and methods of the Node interface.

The Node interface has the following properties:

- attributes—Read-only, of type NamedNodeList

- childNodes—Read-only, of type NodeList

- firstChild—Read-only, of type Node

- lastChild—Read-only, of type Node

- localName—Read-only, of type String

- namespaceURI—Read-only, of type String

- nextSibling—Read-only, of type Node

- nodeName—Read-only, of type String

- nodeType—Read-only, of type Number

- nodeValue—Of type String

- ownerDocument—Read-only, of type Document

- parentNode—Read-only, of type Node

- prefix—Of type String

- previousSibling—Read-only, of type Node

The Node interface has the following methods:

- appendChild(*newChild*)—Returns a Node object

- cloneNode(*deep*)—Returns a Node object

- hasAttributes()—Returns a Boolean value

- hasChildNodes()—Returns a Boolean value

- insertBefore(*newChild*, *refChild*)—Returns a Node object

- isSupported(*feature*, *value*)—Returns a Boolean value

- `normalize()`—Has no return value
- `replaceChild(newChild, oldChild)`—Returns a `Node` object
- `removeChild(oldChild)`—Returns a `Node` object

The `NodeList` Interface

The child nodes of the `Document` node implement the `NodeList` interface.

The `NodeList` interface has the `length` property, which is a read-only property of type `Number`. The `NodeList` interface has the `item(index)` method, which returns a `Node` object.

The `NamedNodeMap` Interface

You can locate the attributes of an element using the `NamedNodeMap` interface.

The `NamedNodeMap` interface has the `length` property, a read-only property of type `Number`.

The `NamedNodeMap` interface has the following methods, all of which return a `Node` object:

- `getNamedItem(name)`
- `getNamedItemNS(namespaceURI,localName)`
- `item(index)`
- `removeNamedItem(name)`
- `removeNamedItemNS(namespaceURI,localName)`
- `setNamedItem(arg)`
- `setNamedItemNS(namespaceURI,localName)`

Before looking in more detail at the interfaces in Figure 16.1, you will look briefly at generally relevant interfaces.

The DOMImplementation Interface

The DOMImplementation interface has no properties, but it does provide methods that allow a programmer to determine what is supported by that implementation.

The hasFeature(*feature, version*) method returns a Boolean value enabling you to test the availability of particular features. The createDocument(*namespaceURI, qualifiedName, doctype*) method enables you to create a new XML document. The createDocumentType(*qualifiedName, publicId, systemId*) method enables you to create a new DOCTYPE declaration.

The DOMException Interface

Several programming languages use a concept called an *exception* to handle errors that occur while a program is running. The DOM provides a DOMException interface. An exception is often said to be *thrown* and is *caught* by an *exception handler.*

The DOMException interface has a single code property, which is of type number. The value of the code property corresponds to the type of exception that has been raised. When programming, you should consider the likely types of errors that might occur and provide error-handling code that provides appropriate responses to those problems.

DOM Interfaces Properties and Methods

Because of space constraints, this section looks at the properties and methods of selected interfaces only.

The Document Interface

The Document interface represents an XML document. The Document interface has the following properties:

- `doctype`—Read-only, of type `DocumentType`

- `implementation`—Read-only, of type `DOMImplementation`

- `documentElement`—Of type `Element`

The methods of the `Document` interface can be used to create new parts of an XML document or to retrieve information about the document. The `Document` interface has the following methods:

- `createAttribute(name)`—Returns an `Attr` object

- `createAttributeNS(namespaceURI, qualifiedName)`—Returns an `Attr` object

- `createCDATASection(data)`—Returns a `CDATASection` object

- `createComment(data)`—Returns a `Comment` object

- `createDocumentFragment()`—Returns a `DocumentFragment` object

- `createElement(tagName)`—Returns an `Element` object

- `createElementNS(namespaceURI, qualifiedName)`—Returns an `Element` object

- `createEntityReference(name)`—Returns an `EntityReference` object

- `createProcessingInstruction(target,data)`—Returns a `ProcessingInstruction` object

- `createTextNode(data)`—Returns a `Text` object

- `getElementsByTagName(tagname)`—Returns a `NodeList` object

- `getElementsByTagNameNS(namespaceURI, localName)`—Returns a `NodeList` object

- `importNode(importedNode, deep)`—Returns a `Node` object

The DocumentType Interface

The DocumentType interface is the DOM representation of the DOCTYPE declaration.

The DocumentType interface has the following properties:

- entities—Read-only, of type NamedNodeMap
- internalSubset—Read-only, of type String
- name—Read-only, of type String
- notations—Read-only, of type NamedNodeMap
- publicId—Read-only, of type String
- systemId— Read-only, of type String

The Element Interface

The Element interface represents an element in an XML document.

The Element interface has the tagName property, which is a read-only property of type String.

The Element interface has the following methods:

- getAttribute(name)—Returns a value of type String
- getAttributeNS(namespaceURI, localName)—Returns a value of type String
- getAttributeNode(name)—Returns a value of type Attr
- getAttributeNodeNS(namespaceURI, localName)—Returns a value of type Attr
- getElementsByTagName(tagname)—Returns a NodeList object
- getElementsByTagNameNS(namespaceURI,localName)—Returns a NodeList object
- hasAttribute(name)—Returns a value of type Boolean

- `hasAttributeNS(`*namespaceURI, localName*`)`—Returns a value of type `Boolean`
- `removeAttribute(`*name*`)`—Returns no value
- `removeAttributeNode(`*oldAttr*`)`—Returns a value of type `Attr`
- `removeAttributeNS(`*namespaceURI, localName*`)`—Returns no value
- `setAttribute(`*name,value*`)`—Returns no value
- `setAttributeNode(`*newAttr*`)`—Returns a value of type `Attr`
- `setAttributeNodeNS(newAttr)`—Returns a value of type `Attr`
- `setAttributeNS(`*namespaceURI, localName*`)`—Returns no value

The `Attr` Interface

The `Attr` interface is the DOM representation of an attribute in an XML document.

The `Attr` interface has the following properties:

- `name`—Read-only, of type `String`
- `ownerElement`—Read-only, of type `Element`
- `specified`—Read-only, of type `Boolean`
- `value`—Of type `String`

The `Attr` interface has no methods specific to it.

The `CharacterData` Interface

The `CharacterData` interface is intended to contain character data. The `Comment` and `Text` interfaces extend the `CharacterData` interface.

The `CharacterData` interface has the following properties:

- `data`—Of type `String`
- `length`—Read-only, of type `Number`

The CharacterData interface has the following methods:

- appendData(*arg*)—Has no return value
- deleteData(*offset, count*)—Has no return value
- insertData(*offset, arg*)—Has no return value
- replaceData(*offset, count, arg*)—Has no return value
- substringData(*offset, count*)—Returns a value of type String

The Text Interface

The Text interface has no properties specific to it.

The Text interface has the splitText(*offset*) method, which returns a Text object.

In Chapter 17 you will create some examples using DOM properties and methods.

Summary

In this lesson, you were introduced to the DOM Level 2. The chapter also discussed the concept of an interface and how an interface can be *extended*. In addition, you learned about the DOM Node interface and DOM interfaces, many of which extend the Node interface.

LESSON 17

The Document Object Model—2

In this lesson, you will see examples of using the Document Object Model to create, retrieve, and manipulate parts of XML documents.

In the examples in this chapter, you will use SVG, which was introduced in Chapter 15, "Presenting XML Graphically—SVG," as an example of an XML application language. SVG has a number of extensions to the core XML DOM, but you won't use any of those to manipulate the DOM. Our purpose is to demonstrate the properties and methods of the XML DOM Level 2 Core, all of which are available in SVG 1.0.

In each of the following examples, the programming language used is JavaScript because many Web developers already have some experience using it. Similar techniques can be applied using Java or other programming languages.

Creating a New Element

The DOM provides more than one way to create an element. You will examine some options in the examples that follow.

Using the `createElement()` Method

In this example, you will create a new SVG element using the `createElement()` method of the `Document` interface. You also will set the values of the attributes of the newly created element.

Listing 17.1 shows the code. Apart from the `circle` element that you will create using the DOM, the SVG document would be blank.

LISTING 17.1 CreateCircle.svg: Creating a `circle` Element Using the DOM

```
<?xml version='1.0'?>
<!DOCTYPE svg PUBLIC "-//W3C//DTD SVG 1.0//EN"
"http://www.w3.org/TR/2001/REC-SVG-20010904/DTD/svg10.dtd">
<svg onload="Initialize(evt)">
<script type="text/javascript" >
<![CDATA[
var SVGDoc;
var SVGRoot;
var myCircle;
function Initialize(){
SVGDoc = evt.getTarget().getOwnerDocument();
SVGRoot = SVGDoc.getDocumentElement();
createCircle(evt);
}

function createCircle(){
myCircle = SVGDoc.createElement("circle");
myCircle.setAttribute("cx", "50px");
myCircle.setAttribute("cy", "50px");
myCircle.setAttribute("r", "30px");
myCircle.setAttribute("style", "fill:none;
   stroke:red; stroke-width:3");
SVGRoot.appendChild(myCircle);
}
]]>
</script>

</svg>
```

The `onload` attribute of the `svg` element calls the `Initialize()` function when the document loads.

Notice that the content of the `script` element is enclosed in a CDATA section to inform the parser that the content should not be treated as XML suitable for parsing.

The new `circle` element is created using the `createElement()` method of the `Document` node in the following line of code:

```
myCircle = SVGDoc.createElement("circle");
```

The `circle` element node exists, but it does not yet have any values for its attributes. The following lines of code use the `setAttribute()` method of the `Element` node to assign values to the attributes of the `circle` element that define the position of its center (`cx` and `cy` attributes), its radius (`r` attribute), and its style (`style` attribute):

```
myCircle.setAttribute("cx", "50px");
myCircle.setAttribute("cy", "50px");
myCircle.setAttribute("r", "30px");
myCircle.setAttribute("style", "fill:none; stroke:red;
  stroke-width:3");
```

You have successfully created the `circle` element and set its attribute values. Finally, you need to append the newly created element as a child of the `Element` node that represents the `svg` document element. This is done using the `appendChild()` method of the `Node` interface:

```
SVGRoot.appendChild(myCircle);
```

Figure 17.1 shows the onscreen appearance when Listing 17.1 is run.

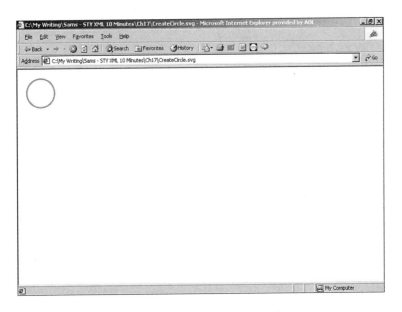

FIGURE 17.1 A `circle` element created using the `createElement()` method.

Using the `createElementNS()` Method

When you have a document in which XML namespaces are not being used or in which a single namespace is using a default namespace declaration, you can use the `createElement()` method to create new elements. If you have documents in which namespace prefixes are used or in which multiple namespaces are (or might be) in use, it makes sense to remove any doubt and use the `createElementNS()` method. This makes it absolutely clear what namespace the newly created element belongs to.

Listing 17.2 shows an example that creates an SVG `rect` element. This creates a rectangle onscreen. However, because all SVG elements in this example use the namespace prefix `svg`, you have to use the `createElementNS()` method to produce the rectangle shape.

LISTING 17.2   CreateRectNS.svg: Using the `createElementNS()` Method to Create a Rectangle

```
<?xml version='1.0'?>
<!DOCTYPE svg PUBLIC "-//W3C//DTD SVG 1.0//EN"
"http://www.w3.org/TR/2001/REC-SVG-20010904/DTD/svg10.dtd">
<svg:svg
 xmlns:svg="http://www.w3.org/2000/svg"
 onload="Initialize(evt)">
<svg:script type="text/javascript" >
<![CDATA[
var SVGDoc;
var SVGRoot;
var myRectangle;
function Initialize(){
SVGDoc = evt.getTarget().getOwnerDocument();
SVGRoot = SVGDoc.getDocumentElement();
createRectangle(evt);
}

function createRectangle(){
myRectangle = SVGDoc.createElementNS
  ➥("http://www.w3.org/2000/svg", "rect");
myRectangle.setAttribute("x", "50px");
myRectangle.setAttribute("y", "50px");
myRectangle.setAttribute("width", "300px");
myRectangle.setAttribute("height", "100px");
myRectangle.setAttribute("style", "fill:#CCCCCC;
  stroke:green; stroke-width:4");
```

LISTING 17.2   Continued

```
SVGRoot.appendChild(myRectangle);
}
]]>
</svg:script>

</svg>
```

The `createElementNS()` method has two arguments. The first is the namespace URI for the element that is to be created. The second argument is the local part of the QName for the element. The namespace URI for SVG 1.0 is www.w3.org/2000/svg.

Notice that it isn't necessary to specify the namespace prefix in the call to the `createElementNS()` method. The namespace URI is already associated with a namespace prefix by means of the namespace declaration `xmlns:svg="http://www.w3.org/2000/svg"` contained in the start tag of the `svg:svg` document element.

Figure 17.2 shows the onscreen appearance when Listing 17.2 is run.

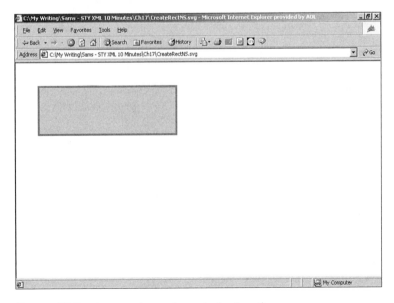

FIGURE 17.2   A `rect` element created using the `createElementNS()` method.

Retrieving Information from the DOM

In earlier examples in this chapter, you created elements and set values for attributes belonging to newly created elements. You can also access information already contained in the DOM and use it for additional purposes.

The `DocumentType` Interface's Properties

If you want to retrieve the information contained in the DOCTYPE declaration, you can access and process the properties of the `DocumentType` object. Listing 17.3 shows an example.

LISTING 17.3   DoctypeProps.svg: Retrieving and Displaying the `DocumentType` Object's Properties

```
<?xml version='1.0'?>
<!DOCTYPE svg PUBLIC "-//W3C//DTD SVG 1.0//EN"
"http://www.w3.org/TR/2001/REC-SVG-20010904/DTD/svg10.dtd">
<svg:svg
 xmlns:svg="http://www.w3.org/2000/svg"
 onload="Initialize(evt)">
<svg:script type="text/javascript" >
<![CDATA[
var SVGDoc;
var SVGRoot;
var SVGDoctype;
function Initialize(){
SVGDoc = evt.getTarget().getOwnerDocument();
SVGRoot = SVGDoc.getDocumentElement();
SVGDoctype = SVGDoc.doctype;
getDoctype(evt);
}

function getDoctype(){
var docElem = SVGDoctype.name;
var firstString = "The document element is: " + docElem;
var firstText = SVGDoc.getElementById("docelem");
var stars = firstText.firstChild;
stars.replaceData(0,5, firstString);

var docPubID = SVGDoctype.publicId;
var secondString = "The public identifier is: " + docPubID;
```

LISTING 17.3 Continued

```
var secondText = SVGDoc.getElementById("pub");
var stars2 = secondText.firstChild;
stars2.replaceData(0,5, secondString);

var docSystID = SVGDoctype.systemId;
var thirdString = "The system identifier is: " + docSystID;
var thirdText = SVGDoc.getElementById("syst");
var stars3 = thirdText.firstChild;
stars3.replaceData(0,5, thirdString);
}
]]>
</svg:script>
<text id="docelem" x="20" y="40">
***
</text>
<text id="pub" x="20" y="100">
***
</text>
<text id="syst" x="20" y="160">
***
</text>
</svg:svg>
```

In the `Initialize()` function, the `SVGDoctype` variable is assigned the value of the `doctype` property of the `SVGDoc` variable. So, the `SVGDoctype` variable is a `DocumentType` object. Therefore, you can retrieve the values of various properties of the `DocumentType` object.

When you call the `getDoctype()` function, you retrieve each of three properties of the `DocumentType` object. You use the value that they contain to replace the data in a `Text` object (which extends a `CharacterData` object) that is a child node of each of three SVG `text` elements. Let's look in detail at the first of these.

This code declares a variable named `docElem` and assigns to it the value of the `name` property of the `SVGDoctype` variable (which itself contains the value of the `doctype` property of the `Document` object):

```
var docElem = SVGDoctype.name;
```

This assigns the element type name of the document element to the docElem variable.

Then you declare a variable firstString and create a message for display that incorporates the value of the docElem variable:

```
var firstString = "The document element is: " + docElem;
```

Then you use the getElementById() method of the Document object to uniquely retrieve the Element node corresponding to the SVG text element with an id attribute of the value docelem.

```
var firstText = SVGDoc.getElementById("docelem");
```

Next declare a stars variable and assign it the value of the firstChild property (a property of the Element interface) of the firstText variable (the first SVG text element, identified by its id attribute):

```
var stars = firstText.firstChild;
```

Finally, you use the replaceData() method of the CharacterData interface to replace the three stars, which is the original content of the text element.

```
stars.replaceData(0,5, firstString);
```

A similar process is carried out for each of the other two text elements. When the document loads, the script instantly replaces the asterisks with three messages that display the values of the name, publicId, and systemId properties of the DocumentType interface. Figure 17.3 shows the onscreen appearance.

Displaying a List of Child Nodes

In this example, you will retrieve information about the NodeList object. This object contains information about the child nodes of the node that represents the svg element in Listing 17.4.

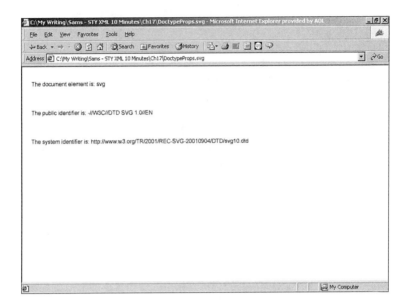

FIGURE 17.3   Displaying properties of the DocumentType interface.

LISTING 17.4   ChildNodes.svg: Retrieving Information About Child Nodes

```
<?xml version='1.0'?>
<!DOCTYPE svg PUBLIC "-//W3C//DTD SVG 1.0//EN"
"http://www.w3.org/TR/2001/REC-SVG-20010904/DTD/svg10.dtd">
<svg
 xmlns:svg="http://www.w3.org/2000/svg"
 onload="Initialize(evt)">
<script type="text/javascript" >
<![CDATA[
var SVGDoc;
var SVGRoot;
var SVGDoctype;
function Initialize(){
SVGDoc = evt.getTarget().getOwnerDocument();
SVGRoot = SVGDoc.getDocumentElement();
SVGDoctype = SVGDoc.doctype;
getChildNodes(evt);
}
```

LISTING 17.4   Continued

```
function getChildNodes(){
var Length = SVGRoot.childNodes.length;
alert("The <svg> element has " + Length + " child nodes.");

for (i=0; i<Length; i++){
if (SVGRoot.childNodes.item(i).nodeType==1){
alert("At position " + i + " in the NodeList object
  is a <" + SVGRoot.childNodes.item(i).tagName + ">
  element.");
} // end if

} // end for loop
} // end getChildNodes() function
]]>
</script>
<text id="first" x="20" y="40">
This is the first &lt;text&gt; element.
</text>
<text id="second" x="20" y="100">
This is the second &lt;text&gt; element.
</text>
<text id="third" x="20" y="160">
This is the third &lt;text&gt; element.
</text>
<rect x="20" y="200" width="200" height="50"
  style="stroke:red; stroke-width:4; fill:none;" />
</svg>
```

Before considering the explanation of how the code works, first look at
the output of the code onscreen. Figures 17.4 and 17.5 show two of the
alert boxes produced by the code. First, you might be surprised by the
first alert box shown in Figure 17.4. Why does it say that there are 11
child nodes? If you look carefully at the code, you will see that each element starts on a new line. So, there is a Text node consisting only of
whitespace separating each element.

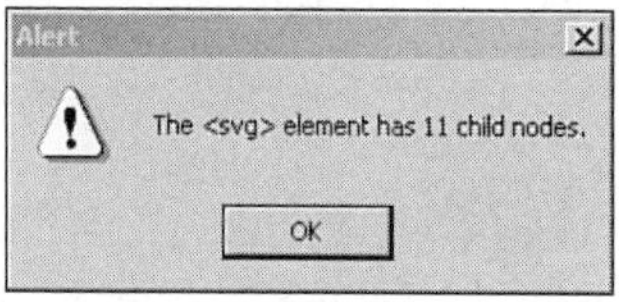

FIGURE 17.4   An alert box showing the number of child nodes for
the <svg> element.

FIGURE 17.5   An alert box for the <rect> element.

Now look at how the code works. Inside the getChildNodes() function, you declare the Length variable. To the Length variable you assign the length property of the NodeList object that contains information about the child nodes of the document element.

```
var Length = SVGRoot.childNodes.length;
```

Next, you use the JavaScript alert() function to output the value of the Length variable:

```
alert("The <svg> element has " + Length + " child nodes.");
```

Then you use a for loop to iterate through the child nodes. The if statement tests whether the value of the nodeType property retrieved by the item() method of the NodeList object equals 1. When the value of the nodeType property is 1, you know that it is an Element node. If the node isn't an Element node (because it is whitespace), you do nothing. But when the value of the nodeType property indicates that the node is an Element node, you output the position of the node and its element type name using the tagName property of the Element interface.

```
for (i=0; i<Length; i++){
if (SVGRoot.childNodes.item(i).nodeType==1){
alert("At position " + i + " in the NodeList object is a <" +
  SVGRoot.childNodes.item(i).tagName + "> element.");
} // end if

} // end for loop
} // end getChildNodes() function
```

Summary

In this lesson, you examined examples of using several DOM properties and methods. You learned how to use some DOM methods to create new elements and how to retrieve the values of various DOM properties.

LESSON 18

SAX—The Simple API for XML

In this lesson you will learn about the Simple API for XML, SAX, and the basics of how SAX programming is done.

What SAX Is and How It Differs from DOM

As you learned in Chapter 16, "The Document Object Model," and Chapter 17, "The Document Object Model—2," DOM programming depends on a tree-like hierarchy of nodes that implement a specified number of interfaces. SAX takes a very different approach. It uses *events* that occur during parsing of an XML document, and it doesn't build a tree hierarchy in memory.

SAX programming is often done using either Java or Visual Basic. In this chapter, you will use Java to illustrate how SAX can be coded.

Brief History of SAX

Unlike most of the XML-related topics covered in this book, SAX is not a product of the W3C. It was created by members of the XML-Dev mailing list to fill a perceived gap in available tools in the early days around the time XML 1.0 was finalized. SAX version 1 was completed in May 1998. SAX version 2 was completed in May 2000.

Pro and Cons of SAX

This section discusses a number of issues relating to SAX and its suitability, compared to DOM programming.

Large Documents

To manipulate a document using DOM programming requires the complete in-memory hierarchy of nodes to be built before manipulation using DOM can begin. As document size increases, the time needed to build the in-memory tree increases.

Also, as XML document size increases, the amount of RAM needed to contain the in-memory hierarchy of nodes increases as well. Beyond a certain document size, which varies according to installed RAM and other factors, the amount of memory available will be inadequate and swapping to disk will be needed. As expected, this will cause deterioration in performance.

In principle, SAX is free from this type of memory limitation because events occur during parsing of an XML document and because the appropriate processing in response to those events takes place without the need to create a potentially large in-memory hierarchy.

Programmer Mindset

It is widely accepted that many XML programmers find the concepts of programming using SAX much less natural than using DOM programming. Perhaps that preference is partly because DOM programming is familiar from scripting HTML Web pages. Whatever the cause, many programmers aren't too comfortable using SAX.

Writing code to handle a cascade of events is certainly different from writing typical JavaScript or Java procedural code.

Basics of SAX Programming

SAX programming depends on recognizing events that occur during the process of parsing an XML document.

Parsing Events

In this section, you will use pseudocode to see what happens as an XML document is parsed using a SAX parser.

Listing 18.1 shows a short XML document that you will use to illustrate the SAX approach.

LISTING 18.1   SAXSource.xml: A Short XML Document

```
<?xml version='1.0'?>
<?xml-stylesheet href="myCSS.css" type="text/css" ?>
<!-- This is an XML comment. -->
<myDocument>
Some text content.
</myDocument>
```

A SAX parser would respond to parsing an XML document like this by signaling events, similar to the following:

```
start_document;
processing_instruction;
start_element (<myDocument>);
characters;
end_element (</myDocument>);
end_document;
```

The existence of the XML declaration and the comment are ignored.

Clearly, in anything but a very short document, a very large number of events will be signaled. It is up to the programmer to write code to define what to do in response to all such events.

SAX 2 Interfaces

When discussing the Document Object Model, we defined an interface as a specified grouping of properties and methods. SAX uses the following important interfaces:

- ContentHandler—Defines methods that process XML document content

- DTDHandler—Defines methods that process DTDs

- ErrorHandler—Defines methods that process errors

These interfaces are implemented by classes in SAX parsers.

Installing a SAX Parser

To run a Java SAX-capable parser, you need the following installed on your computer:

- A Java Software Development Kit, version 1.1 or higher.
- A SAX2-compatible XML parser installed on your Java CLASSPATH.
- A SAX2 distribution on your Java CLASSPATH. This would likely be included with the SAX2-compatible XML parser.

Installing the JSDK

You might already have a JSDK installed. If not, you can download a JSDK from http://java.sun.com/j2se/. The URL gives you access to information about the Standard Edition of Java—j2se.

You can check if you have a JSDK installed by searching for a file named javac.exe. If javac.exe is present, you have a JSDK (formerly called a JDK) installed. Up to Java version 1.3, you might find javac.exe in a directory named something like c:\jdk1.3.1\bin. In Java 2 version 1.4, you will find it in a directory named something like c:\j2sdk1.4\bin.

Download the JSDK appropriate to your operating system and install it according to the instructions supplied by Sun.

Take note of the exact name of the directory that you install the JSDK into. You will add that to your computer's path environment variable in a moment.

Installing the Xerces Parser

Information about the Java version of the Xerces 2 XML parser is located at http://xml.apache.org/xerces2-j/index.html. From the Downloads link, select the latest stable version of the Xerces-J parser appropriate to your operating system.

When the download has completed, install the Xerces-J parser to a directory. We installed Xerces-J in c:\Xerces-J2.0.2.

Setting path and CLASSPATH Environment Variables

Your computer needs to be capable of locating the Java programs and the Xerces parser.

The directory into which you installed the JSDK must be added to the path environment variable. In Windows 2000, go to the Control Panel and select the System option. The System Properties window should open. Select the Advanced tab. Click the Environment Variables button halfway down the page. Scroll down the list of System Variables until the path variable is highlighted. Click the Edit button. A window will open with the current value of the path variable.

Your current path might be something like this:

```
c:\WINNT\system32;c:\WINNT
```

You need to add the directory where the JSDK is installed. In my case, the JSDK is in c:\j2sdk1.4.0\bin, so that is added to the existing value of the path variable, separated by a semicolon from the existing value.

```
c:\WINNT\system32;c:\WINNT;c:\j2sdk1.4.0\bin
```

> **Caution** Check if another Java installation already exists in the path variable. If so, you might want to simply use that. Having more than one Java installation specified in the path environment variable is a recipe for problems.

If you have done no Java programming on your computer, you will likely have to create a new CLASSPATH environment variable. Otherwise, edit the existing CLASSPATH environment variable to add c:\Xerces-J2.0.2 (or the directory you installed Xerces in) to it, separated by a semicolon from any existing paths.

> **Tip** If you don't want to permanently change environment variables, create a short batch file that will set the path and CLASSPATH variables from the command line.

You also need to add the Xerces-J version 2 jar files to the CLASSPATH—xercesImpl.jar and xmlParserAPIs.jar.

Now that we've discussed a number of issues about how to use SAX, let's move on and use a Java example to illustrate the basics of how SAX can be used.

Simple SAX Example

This example creates a Java program that you can run from the command line. You will be able to specify an XML document to be parsed, and messages will be output onscreen in response to events generated by the SAX parser.

> **Note** Java, like XML, is case sensitive. All names of interfaces, classes, and so on in the following code must use the correct case if your application is to run correctly.

Listing 18.2 shows a simple SAX example.

LISTING 18.2 myHandler.java: A Java Program That Provides Screen Output in Response to SAX Events

```
import org.xml.sax.XMLReader;
import org.xml.sax.SAXException;
import org.xml.sax.Attributes;
import org.xml.sax.helpers.DefaultHandler;
import org.xml.sax.helpers.XMLReaderFactory;

import org.apache.xerces.parsers.SAXParser;
```

LISTING 18.2   Continued

```java
public class myHandler extends DefaultHandler
{
  public static void main(String[] argv) throws Exception {
  if (argv.length == 0) {
  System.out.println("You need to specify a file name");
  System.exit(0);
  }
  System.out.println("The program myHandler has started ...");
  myHandler reader = new myHandler();
  reader.read(argv[0]);
  }

  public void read(String fileName) throws Exception{
  System.out.println("read() method entered ...");
  XMLReader parser = XMLReaderFactory.createXMLReader();

  parser.setContentHandler(this);
  parser.parse(fileName);
  }

  public void startDocument() throws SAXException {
  System.out.println("The document has been opened.");
  }

  public void processingInstruction(String target,
   String data) throws SAXException {
  System.out.println("A processing instruction with target,
   " +target+ " and data " +data+ ".");
  }

  public void startElement(String uri, String localName,
    String QName, Attributes attributes) throws SAXException{
  System.out.println("Start tag of element "
   + localName + " was found.");
  }

   public void endElement(String uri, String localName,
     String QName) throws SAXException{
  System.out.println("End tag of element "
   + localName + " was found.");
  }

  public void characters(char[] characters, int start,
   int length) throws SAXException {
```

LISTING 18.2   Continued

```
System.out.println("Character content encountered.");
}

public void endDocument() throws SAXException {
    System.out.println("The document has been completed.");
}

}
```

The Java file must be compiled. Using the javac compiler, you can issue this command to create a class file:

```
javac myHandler.java
```

To run the class file, issue this command:

```
java -Dorg.xml.sax.driver=org.apache.xerces.parsers.SAXParser
    myHandler SAXSource.xml
```

That command assigns the class org.apache.xerces.parsers.SAXParser to the environment variable org.xml.sax.driver.

When the code is run, you will see an onscreen appearance like that shown in Figure 18.1.

Let's look briefly at what the code does.

You first create a class called myHandler. The main() method accepts string arguments. So, when you enter the following command, the SAXSource.xml is the sole string argument.

```
java -Dorg.xml.sax.driver=org.apache.xerces.parsers.SAXParser
    myHandler SAXSource.xml
```

This next if statement checks to see if a filename has been supplied as an argument:

```
if (argv.length == 0) {
System.out.println("You need to specify a file name");
System.exit(0);
```

If no filename is supplied, an error message is output and the program exits.

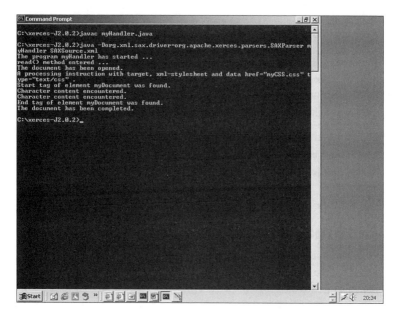

FIGURE 18.1   The output when the `myHandler` class is run.

This code indicates that the program has started successfully:

```
System.out.println("The program myHandler has started ...");
```

The `read()` method creates an `XMLReader` that parses the file supplied in the argument at the command line.

The parser raises events at many points as it parses the document. The `startDocument()` method outputs a message when the start of the document has been encountered. Then when the `<?xml-stylesheet ?>` processing instruction is encountered, the `processingInstruction()` method outputs a message that tells what the `target` and `data` of the processing instruction are.

When the start of the `myDocument` element is found, the `startElement()` method is called and a message is output. When the character content of the `myDocument` element is encountered, the `characters()` method is called and outputs a message.

Finally, the endElement() and endDocument() methods are called and appropriate messages are output to the screen.

In this short example, when each of the methods of the org.xml.sax.helpers.DefaultHandler interface is called as a result of the appropriate event happening during parsing, we have simply output a message to the screen that says what event(s) has been encountered.

Of course, in more serious use of SAX, the way in which you implement an interface is very flexible, and you can write Java code to do whatever is appropriate in response to particular events encountered by the SAX parser.

Summary

This lesson introduced you to the Simple API for XML, SAX. It described the event-based approach of SAX and gave an example to demonstrate simple usage of SAX.

LESSON 19

Beyond DTDs—W3C XML Schema

In this chapter, you will learn about W3C XML Schema, an alternative technology to Document Type Definitions (DTDs) described in Chapter 4, "Valid XML—Document Type Definitions."

W3C XML Schema Basics

W3C XML Schema is a schema-definition language expressed in XML syntax. To avoid ambiguity, W3C XML Schema is often referred to as *XSD Schema* because in an earlier version it was called XML Schema Definition Language. Recently, the abbreviation WXS has also come into use to refer to the W3C XML Schema language.

 Note Other schema languages are expressed in XML syntax, such as RELAX NG (a combination of TREX and RELAX) and XDR (XML Data Reduced, from Microsoft).

In this section, you are introduced to some of the reasons why W3C XML Schema was developed as an alternative schema mechanism to the Document Type Definition (DTD).

 Note The W3C XML Schema specification is lengthy and very complex. This chapter can give you only an indication of some straightforward W3C XML Schema structures.

Limitations of DTDs

DTDs were inherited by XML from the Standard Generalized Markup Language (SGML). SGML was (and is) commonly used for document-centric data storage such as very large documents, including technical manuals. A DTD that describes most data as #PCDATA is adequate for many document-centric purposes because one piece of text is pretty much like another—simply a sequence of characters.

However, for many uses of XML to store data that might otherwise be stored in a relational or other type of database-management system, you will likely want to say more about the *type* of pieces of data that an element can contain.

> A piece of data conforms to a *type* if the characters it contains express a defined idea. For example, you might have a date type as the allowed content of an element. If the characters contained were 2002/12/25, using an internationally recognized date format convention, you can interpret that as a date. If the element contained the characters $100.50, you would conclude that the type of the data contained in the element didn't conform to a date type.

In a DTD, when mixed content was allowed, very few constraints could be imposed on the allowed content. For example, using a DTD, with mixed content it isn't possible to impose a defined order on elements. W3C XML Schema provides greater control in this situation.

W3C XML Schema also gives greater control over how many occurrences of an element are allowed. For example, it allows you to define that an element occurs at least twice and at most five times:

```
<xsd:element name="someName" minOccurs="2" maxOccurs="5" />
```

You can't do that in a DTD.

W3C XML Schema also specifies many additional datatypes for element content, and so on. W3C XML Schema has many built-in datatypes and also allows you to create your own, for example, by restricting allowed content to enumerated values or values defined by a regular expression.

W3C XML Schema Jargon

Let's look briefly at some terminology. A W3C XML Schema document defines the allowed content for a *class* of XML documents. A single document of that class is called an *instance document*.

Elements and attributes are said to be *declared* in a W3C XML Schema document. The content of elements and attributes has a *type*, which can be either of *simple type* or *complex type*. Types can be built-in (that is, they are defined in the W3C XML Schema specification itself) or can be *defined* by a schema developer. Elements and attributes have *declarations*. Simple types and complex types have *definitions*.

> **Note** Typically, anything but very simple schemas are created semi-automatically by programs such as XML Spy. The examples shown in this chapter are intended to show you basic structures within a W3C XML Schema.

Declaring Elements

In W3C XML Schema terminology, elements and attributes are *declared*. Both elements and attributes can occur in an instance document.

Listing 19.1 shows a simple example of an XML instance document. Listing 19.2 shows a W3C XML Schema document against which Listing 19.1 can be validated.

LISTING 19.1 BasicDocument.xml: A Short XML Instance
Document

```
<?xml version="1.0"?>
<basicDocument>
Some text content.
</basicDocument>
```

LISTING 19.2 BasicDocument.xsd: A Schema for Listing 19.1

```
<?xml version='1.0'?>
<xsd:schema xmlns:xsd="http://www.w3.org/2001/XMLSchema">
<xsd:element name="basicDocument" type="xsd:string" />
</xsd:schema>
```

The indicative namespace prefix in the W3C XML Schema document is
xsd. The namespace declaration in the start tag of the xsd:schema element
associates the xsd namespace prefix with the namespace URI
www.w3.org/2001/XMLSchema.

An xsd:element element is used to declare the basicDocument element
that is found in the instance document. The content of the basicDocument
element is text content only and is declared, using the type attribute of the
xsd:element element, to be of type xsd:string. The xsd:string type is
one of many built-in types specified in the W3C XML Schema
Recommendations.

If you have a slightly more complex instance document, such as the one
in Listing 19.3, you must make use of a complex type definition as well
as an element declaration.

LISTING 19.3 LessBasicDocument.xml: An XML Document
with Attributes and Nested Elements

```
<?xml version='1.0'?>
<lessBasicDocument>
 <Person category="celebrity" status="alive">
  <Name>Tiger Woods</Name>
  <Citizenship>United States</Citizenship>
  <Occupation>Professional Golfer</Occupation>
 </Person>
</lessBasicDocument>
```

As you can see, the content of the `lessBasicDocument` element is a hier-archy of nested elements. In addition, the `Person` element has two attrib-utes, `category` and `status`.

Listing 19.4 shows one approach to a schema for Listing 19.3. W3C XML Schema provides flexible tools that allow several approaches to how the structure of an instance document is represented.

LISTING 19.4 LessBasicDocument.xsd: A Schema for Listing 19.3

```
<?xml version='1.0'?>
<xsd:schema xmlns:xsd="http://www.w3.org/2001/XMLSchema">

<xsd:element name="lessBasicDocument" type="myPersonType"/>

<xsd:complexType name="myPersonType">
 <xsd:element name="Person" type="PersonType"/>
</xsd:complexType>

<xsd:complexType name="PersonType">
 <xsd:sequence>
  <xsd:element name="Name" type="xsd:string" />
  <xsd:element name="Citizenship" type="xsd:string" />
  <xsd:element name="Occupation" type="OccupationType" />
 </xsd:sequence>
 <xsd:attribute name="category" type="xsd:string" />
 <xsd:attribute name="status" type="StatusType" />
</xsd:complexType>

<xsd:simpleType name="OccupationType">
 <xsd:restriction base="xsd:string">
  <xsd:enumeration value="Professional Golfer" />
  <xsd:enumeration value="Actor" />
  <xsd:enumeration value="Professional Footballer" />
 </xsd:restriction>
</xsd:simpleType>

<xsd:simpleType name="StatusType">
 <xsd:restriction base="xsd:string">
  <xsd:pattern value="alive|dead" />
 </xsd:restriction>
</xsd:simpleType>

</xsd:schema>
```

The document element is declared using this:

```
<xsd:element name="lessBasicDocument"
type="myPersonType"/>
```

For the allowed content of the lessBasicDocument element, you need to find the definition for the myPersonType complex type:

```
<xsd:complexType name="myPersonType">
 <xsd:element name="Person" type="PersonType"/>
</xsd:complexType>
```

To find the allowed content of the Person element, you need to find the definition of the PersonType complex type:

```
<xsd:complexType name="PersonType">
 <xsd:sequence>
  <xsd:element name="Name" type="xsd:string" />
  <xsd:element name="Citizenship" type="xsd:string" />
  <xsd:element name="Occupation" type="OccupationType" />
 </xsd:sequence>
 <xsd:attribute name="category" type="xsd:string" />
 <xsd:attribute name="status" type="StatusType" />
</xsd:complexType>
```

This definition specifies that a Person element is allowed to have a sequence of child elements, as defined by the content of the xsd:sequence element. The Person element may also have two attributes named category and status.

The values of some elements and attributes are simply strings, as indicated by the xsd:string value for the type attribute. The xsd:string type is one of many built-in datatypes in W3C XML Schema.

The allowed content of the Occupation element is defined in the definition for the OccupationType type:

```
<xsd:simpleType name="OccupationType">
 <xsd:restriction base="xsd:string">
  <xsd:enumeration value="Professional Golfer" />
  <xsd:enumeration value="Actor" />
  <xsd:enumeration value="Professional Footballer" />
 </xsd:restriction>
</xsd:simpleType>
```

The xsd:restriction element is used to restrict (or constrain) allowed values. The base attribute of xsd:restriction indicates the base type that is being restricted. In this case, the base type is xsd:string. The xsd:enumeration element is used to specify allowed values.

An alternative type of restriction uses the xsd:pattern element. The content of the value attribute of xsd:pattern that defines the allowed values can be a single literal value or a choice of values (as in the following code):

```
<xsd:simpleType name="StatusType">
 <xsd:restriction base="xsd:string">
  <xsd:pattern value="alive|dead" />
 </xsd:restriction>
</xsd:simpleType>
```

Or, it can be a regular expression.

Declaring Attributes

To declare an attribute, you use the xsd:attribute element. The name attribute of the xsd:attribute element contains the attribute name. The value of an attribute is always a simple type. If the permitted values of the attribute are restricted, the xsd:simpleType element is used with the xsd:restriction child element to constrain the permitted values of the attribute.

Declaration of an attribute inside an xsd:complexType element was shown in Listing 19.4. An alternate approach is to declare the attribute inside an element declaration:

```
<xsd:element name="Person">
 <xsd:complexType >
  <xsd:sequence>
   <xsd:element name="Name" type="xsd:string" />
   <xsd:element name="Citizenship" type="xsd:string" />
   <xsd:element name="Occupation" type="OccupationType" />
  </xsd:sequence>
  <xsd:attribute name="category" type="xsd:string" />
  <xsd:attribute name="status" type="StatusType" />
 </xsd:complexType>
<xsd:element>
```

Defining Complex and Simple Types

In W3C XML Schema there are two basic types of element content, simple types and complex types.

Simple types contain only text content and have no child elements or any attributes on the element. If an element has one or more attributes or has one or more child elements, it is said to be of complex type.

Defining Simple Types

Suppose you have a document with the following structure:

```
<memo>
<from>John Smith</from>
<email>JSmith@XMML.com</email>
<to>Peter Roehampton</to>
<emailto>Peter@SVGenius.com</emailto>
<message>Hello Peter. I attach the SVG graphic you wanted to
  see.</message>
</memo>
```

Several elements have simple string content of type xsd:string. You can define a simple type, such as for the email element, as in this code, if the allowed content is a built-in W3C XML Schema datatype:

```
<xsd:element name="email" type="xsd:string" />
```

However, you might want to define your own simple type. If you want to constrain allowed values for element content, you can use an anonymous simple type definition (that is, using no name attribute on the xsd:complexType element), like this:

```
<xsd:element name="from">
 <xsd:simpleType>
  <xsd:restriction base="xsd:string">
   <xsd:enumeration value="John Smith" />
   <xsd:enumeration value="Janet Smith" />
  </xsd:restriction>
 </xsd:simpleType>
</xsd:element>
```

The allowed values for the element content are the strings "John Smith" and "Janet Smith". This would ensure that only authorized senders of email could be identified in the from element.

Defining Complex Types

The type of an element that has either element content or attribute(s) or both is of *complex type*. A complex type can be named or anonymous.

A named complex type definition is referenced using the type attribute of an xsd:element element. An anonymous complex type definition is nested inside an xsd:element.

If a sequence of elements is the allowed content, as in this code

```
<parent>
<firstChild>content</firstChild>
<secondChild>more content</secondChild>
</parent>
```

then an xsd:sequence element is nested within the xsd:complexType element and the permitted elements are listed in the allowed order:

```
<xsd:complexType>
 <xsd:sequence>
  <xsd:element name="firstChild" type="xsd:string" />
  <xsd:element name="secondChild" type="xsd:string" />
 </xsd:sequence>
</xsd:complexType>
```

Alternatively, if the allowed structures in the instance document were

```
<parent>
<firstChoice>Some content</firstChoice>
</parent>
```

or

```
<parent>
<secondChoice>Some other content</secondChoice>
</parent>
```

this can be expressed in a schema using the xsd:choice element:

```
<xsd:complexType>
 <xsd:choice>
  <xsd:element name="firstChoice" type="xsd:string" />
  <xsd:element name="secondChoice" type="xsd:string" />
 </xsd:choice>
</xsd:complexType>
```

Much more to W3C XML Schema exists than has been mentioned in this brief introduction. However, the structures illustrated give you a flavor of the syntax of W3C XML Schema.

Summary

This lesson presented some of the reasons why XML developers need something with more functionality than traditional DTDs.

You learned how to declare elements and attributes in W3C XML Schema, and you also learned how to define W3C XML Schema simple types and complex types.

APPENDIX A
XML Online Resources

The number of online XML-related resources is huge and growing. This appendix lists some resources that you might find useful as you look to build on the knowledge you have gained in *Sams Teach Yourself XML in 10 Minutes*.

Web Sites

Web sites with useful XML information abound. This section can list only a few.

The World Wide Web Consortium

The World Wide Web Consortium (W3C) published the XML 1.0 Recommendation and a large number of associated specifications for languages created in XML or, like XPath, in non-XML syntax but designed to be used with XML documents.

All W3C technical documents—full Recommendations and non-final versions of specifications—can be accessed at www.w3.org/TR/.

The following list contains URLs that will take you directly to selected W3C Recommendations for some of the XML technologies discussed in this book.

- The XML 1.0 Recommendation (2nd Edition)—
  www.w3.org/TR/2000/REC-xml-20001006

- The Namespaces in XML Recommendation—
  www.w3.org/TR/REC-xml-names-19990114

- The Associating Stylesheets with XML Documents 1.0 Recommendation—www.w3.org/1999/06/REC-xml-stylesheet-19990629

- The XML Path Language (XPath) Version 1.0— www.w3.org/TR/1999/REC-xpath-19991116

- XSL Transformations (XSLT) Version 1.0— www.w3.org/TR/1999/REC-xslt-19991116

- The Document Object Model (DOM) Level 2 Core Specification—www.w3.org/TR/2000/REC-DOM-Level-2-Core-20001113

- The Document Object Model (DOM) Level 2 Events Specification—www.w3.org/TR/2000/REC-DOM-Level-2-Events-20001113

- Scalable Vector Graphics (SVG) 1.0 Specification— www.w3.org/TR/2001/REC-SVG-20010904/

- XML Linking Language (XLink) Version 1.0— www.w3.org/TR/2001/REC-xlink-20010627/

- XPointer Framework—www.w3.org/TR/xptr-framework/

- XPointer xpointer() Scheme—www.w3.org/TR/xptr-xpointer/

- XPointer xmlns() Scheme—www.w3.org/TR/xptr-xmlns/

- XPointer element() Scheme—www.w3.org/TR/xptr-element/

- XML Schema Part 1: Structures—www.w3.org/TR/2001/REC-xmlschema-1-20010502/

- XML Schema Part 2: Datatypes—www.w3.org/TR/2001/REC-xmlschema-2-20010502/

In addition to the specification documents for the individual technologies discussed in this book, the W3C site provides Web pages that describe ongoing developments, available tools, and other useful information.

These pages can be accessed from the menu of choices at the left of the W3C home page at http://www.w3.org/.

XML.com

XML.com is a general XML Web site that includes tutorial articles and general discussion of an extensive range of XML-related topics. XML.com is an excellent site that many people with more than a passing interest in the XML family of technologies visit regularly.

XMLHack.com

The XMLHack.com Web site covers many news-related XML items. It has an archive of news items browsable by subject. Visitors can subscribe to an announcement mailing list giving information on the latest news items and developments on the XMLHack.com Web site.

The Apache XML Web Site

The Apache Foundation has several active XML projects. Information on those projects can be accessed at http://xml.apache.org/.

Google

At http://groups.google.com/, you can access Usenet discussions on numerous topics, including XML.

SVGSpider.com

Now showing its age, http://www.SVGSpider.com is the world's first continuing all-SVG Web site. Other example all-SVG sites can be viewed at http://www.XMML.com and http://www.EditITWrite.com.

Mailing Lists

Many mailing lists are devoted to general or very specific XML-related topics.

The XML-DEV Mailing List

The XML-DEV mailing list is very active and includes discussions of any XML-related topic. The level of discussion tends to be fairly high. It isn't typically a good place to ask beginner questions. To subscribe, send an email to xml-dev-request@lists.xml.org with the word **Subscribe** in the subject line.

The XSL Mailing List

The XSL mailing list is hosted at http://www.mulberrytech.com/ xsl/xsl-list/index.html. The XSLT community is a large and active one, and the volume of posts on the XSL list can be overwhelming at times.

The XSLTalk Mailing List

Hosted at www.yahoogroups.com/group/XSLTalk, this mailing list tends to have a Microsoft flavor to its discussions.

The SVG-Developers Mailing List

Despite reaching W3C Recommendation status as recently as September 2001, SVG has a very active developers' mailing list hosted at http://www.yahoogroups.com/group/svg-developers/. Subscription information is available at the site.

The SVG-Developers mailing list is also a very active mailing list, with posts often exceeding 30 per day on a sustained basis.

A mailing list dedicated to the use of SVG on mobile platforms has recently been formed. Further information is located at www.yahoogroups.com/group/SVG-Mobile.

The www-svg Mailing List

The W3C has a mailing list devoted to SVG. Activity tends to focus on details of the SVG specification, and the volume of posts is much lower than on the SVG-Developers mailing list.

W3C XML Schema Mailing Lists

The W3C has a mailing list that you can join by sending an email to xmlschema-dev-request@w3.org with **subscribe** in the subject line.

There is also an XSD Schema mailing list on YahooGroups.com. Details are found at www.yahoogroups.com/group/XSDSchema. To join, send an email to XSDSchema-subscribe@yahoogroups.com.

Appendix B
XML Tools

This appendix describes some XML tools. First, let's look at some XML editors.

XML Editors

Many XML editors are on the market, with varied functionality and varying prices. The absence of a particular editor in this section does not indicate that it is an inappropriate editor for your use.

XML Writer

XML Writer is a basic but very useful XML editor that is easy to use and relatively inexpensive. Further details are available at www.xmlwriter.com/.

XML Writer features syntax color highlighting and can check XML documents for well-formedness and validity. You can create and save document templates. Examples of this include an XSLT stylesheet with a basic HTML document as literal result elements, and an SVG document with the elements already in place for adding JavaScript code.

At the time of this writing, the current version is 1.2.1 and the upcoming release of version 2.0 has been hinted at for a very long time. This delay means that the current version has no support for W3C XML Schemas, although DTDs are well-supported. Screen shots of version 2.0 are now being shown, which are a good sign that a more full-featured version 2.0 is not too far away. In version 2.0, support for W3C XML Schema is promised along with many other improvements.

A 30-day download of XML Writer is available to enable you to test the program's capabilities.

XML Spy

XML Spy is a well-featured XML editor with capabilities that go far beyond the capability to edit XML documents. The higher price of the product reflects its multiple capabilities. The current version at the time of writing is 5.0, and further information is available at www.xmlspy.com.

XML Spy supports XML document editing, either as text or as a logical hierarchy. XML Spy supports XSLT, XML Schema, and XSL-FO, and it also can generate XML from any ODBC-compliant data source. If you use multiple XML languages, you might find XML Spy particularly appropriate to your needs.

A 30-day download is available to enable you to test the capabilities of XML Spy. Given the many aspects of the program, you will likely be able to explore only part of the program in that time.

XSLT Tools

This section describes several commonly used XSLT tools. XML Spy Suite, mentioned in the preceding section, also includes an XSLT Designer.

Saxon and Instant Saxon

Saxon is a Java-based XSLT processor. Instant Saxon is a Windows-specific executable version that can be run on Windows 95, 98, Me, and 2000.

> **Note** If you want to run Instant Saxon on Windows XP, you will need to download the Microsoft Java Virtual Machine, the JVM, separately from the Microsoft Web site. Visit www.microsoft.com/java/default.htm for current information.

The various versions of Saxon—stable and developer versions—and Instant Saxon are described at http://saxon.sourceforge.net.

The full Saxon download contains API documentation and examples, as well as source code. Instant Saxon contains an executable with a single HTML Web page in a Zip file.

> **Caution** Older versions of the Microsoft JVM can cause Saxon to output blank documents. This problem is now not common, but you might want to check that you have the latest version of the JVM using the Windows Update facility in Internet Explorer.

To install Instant Saxon on a Windows platform, assuming that you have WinZip (www.winzip.com) or a similar utility installed, simply double-click the Zip file and select an appropriately named directory (perhaps C:\Instant Saxon) to install Saxon into. To check whether Instant Saxon has installed correctly, open a command prompt, change to the installation directory you chose, and type **Saxon**. The command prompt window should show a message indicating the version of Instant Saxon that you installed and a series of messages explaining the basic syntax for using Instant Saxon. If you see that message, the installation has been successful.

Likely, you will want to store XML and XSLT files in the Instant Saxon directory or add the appropriate directory to the path environment variable.

MSXML

Microsoft started development of an "XSL" processor at a time before XSL (in W3C terminology) split into XSLT and XSL Formatting Objects (XSL-FO).

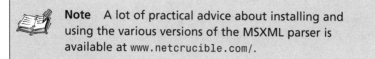

> **Note**   A lot of practical advice about installing and
> using the various versions of the MSXML parser is
> available at www.netcrucible.com/.

MSXML version 3 (and above) includes an XML processor and an XSLT
processor (among other things). If you have Microsoft Internet Explorer
version 5.5 or earlier, you will not have MSXML version 3 installed by
default. Earlier versions of MSXML support a Microsoft-specific, non-
standard approximation of XSLT. Versions of MSXML earlier than 3
should be avoided to ensure future compatibility with W3C standards.

To download the MSXML parser and XSLT processor, visit
www.microsoft.com/XML/.

> **Note**   Microsoft has begun to refer to the MSXML
> software as Microsoft XML Core Services. If you can't
> find any reference to MSXML 3 or 4, search for the
> newer term.

Chris Bayes has written an MSXML Sniffer utility that can detect
whether you have MSXML version 3 or above installed and whether it is
in replace mode (which is what you want for XSLT processing). Go to
www.bayes.co.uk/xml/index.xml?/xml/main.xml and look for the link
to MSXML Sniffer (left panel of the Web page, at the time of writing).

> **Note**   Internet Explorer version 6 has MSXML version
> 3 already installed.

Xalan

Xalan is a Java-based XSLT processor under ongoing development by the
Apache Foundation (http://xml.apache.org). Details of the Java version

of the Xalan XSLT processor can be found at
`http://xml.apache.org/xalan-j/index.html`. At the time of this writing, Xalan-J, the Java version of Xalan, is at version 2.4.

> **Note**   Xalan version 1 is no longer supported and has been removed from the xml.apache.org Web site. If your computer uses only early versions of Java, you might be able to download the necessary files to run Xalan 1 by searching in Google.com.

Xalan can be used from the command line, can be used in an applet or servlet, or can be incorporated in a full application.

By default, Xalan-J uses the Xerces XML parser, also from the Apache Foundation. Typically the Xalan download includes the appropriate version of the Xerces parser. If you want to run Xalan with another XML processor, configuration instructions are available from the Apache Web site.

To run the currently supported versions of Xalan-J and Xerces, you need either a Java Runtime or a Java Software Developer's Kit installed on your computer. Version 1.2 or later is required. If you do not already have a suitable Java Runtime or JSDK installed, you can download one from `http://java.sun.com`. Further information on the latest versions is also available there.

Be sure to add the Xalan and Xerces jar files to the classpath on your computer.

> **Caution**   If you use multiple Java applications that make use of the Xerces XML parser, it is very easy to have multiple versions of Xerces on your computer at one time. If more than one version has been added to the classpath, you might find that the wrong version is accessed first and that unexpected and puzzling errors occur.

> **Tip** If you plan to use multiple Java-based applications, create a simple batch file that you run when you open the command window. The batch file can set the path and classpath to settings that are specific to the Java application that you want to run. This avoids potential clashes between different versions of Java software.

XLink and XPointer Tools

At the time of this writing, XLink and XPointer tools are very limited in number.

The Mozilla 1.0 browser (www.mozilla.org) implements simple XLink links.

The most full-featured XLink processor is the XLiP processor from Fujitsu (www.labs.fujitsu.com/free/xlip/en/), which is a Java application.

At the time of this writing, XLiP was not updated to take into account the July 2002 XPointer working drafts. Despite that, it is the most full-featured XLink and XPointer tool generally available. At the time of this writing, a free evaluation download is available.

XLiP also supports a demo of the Extensible Business Reporting Language, XBRL. To run it, you need the Tomcat server available from http://jakarta.apache.org/tomcat/.

APPENDIX C
XML Glossary

This appendix provides definitions of selected XML-related terms.

arc   XLink construct that provides information about how to traverse a pair of resources.

attribute axis   XPath axis that contains only attribute nodes. The abbreviated syntax for the `attribute` axis is the @ character, usually followed immediately by the attribute name or a wildcard.

axis   XPath term referring to the way in which the in-memory representation of an XML document is navigated.

axis name   The part of a *location step* that specifies which XPath axis is to be used in the location step.

CDATA section   Character data not intended to be parsed by an XML processor is enclosed in a CDATA section.

character encoding   A way to represent a character, or set of characters by one or more numeric values.

character point   Unicode term indicating the numeric representation of a character.

character-point   XPointer `xpointer()` scheme term indicating a point within a container node whose content is character content.

child axis   XPath axis that contains element nodes, comment nodes, processing instruction nodes, and text nodes.

child element   Element that is nested completely within another XML element, which is termed the parent element.

child node   Node in the XPath child axis.

code point   Numeric code for a character in character encodings such as Unicode.

collapsed range XPointer term referring to a range where the start point and the end point are the same point.

complex type One of two types of element content permitted in W3C XML Schemas. An element is said to be of complex type if it has one or more attributes or one or more child elements. An element with only text content is said to be of simple type.

container node XPointer term indicating a node within whose content a point is located.

context XPath term indicating the starting point for interpretation of a location path or expression.

context location XPointer term corresponding to and extending the XPath notion of a context node.

context node XPath term referring to the node that navigation starts from.

covering range XPointer term designating a range that completely encloses a location.

current node XSLT term that often, but not always, refers to the same node as the XPath context node.

deep copy Copy that results from copying an element in an XSLT transformation with its content. The `xsl:copy-of` element is used.

default namespace A namespace name (also called a namespace URI) declared using a namespace declaration of the form `xmlns='namespaceURI'`.

descendant node Node in the XPath `descendant` axis.

DOCTYPE declaration Informal synonym for the Document Type Declaration.

document element Also called the root element. All elements of an XML document are nested between the start tag and end tag of the document element.

Document Object Model A W3C-approved way to model content of XML documents.

document order   XPath term referring to the order in which elements occur in an XML document. A document precedes a second element in document order if the start tag of the element precedes the start tag of the second element.

Document Type Declaration   XML 1.0 construct that expresses the element type name of the document element; references the external subset of the DTD, if one exists; and contains the internal subset of the DTD, if one exists.

Document Type Definition   Often referred to as a DTD. A DTD consists of two parts—the internal subset and the external subset. The internal subset consists of markup declarations that are contained within the DOCTYPE declaration.

DOM   Abbreviation for the Document Object Model.

DTD   Abbreviation for the Document Type Definition.

element content   The content between the start tag and end tag of an element.

element node   In XPath, node that represents an element in the source XML document.

element type name   The name of an element type. The element type name of a <myElement></myElement> tag pair is myElement.

empty element   XML element that has no content. It may be represented by a start tag and end tag pair with no content (not even a single whitespace character in between) or as a shorthand empty element tag, <anEmptyTag/>.

empty element tag   Shorthand form of expressing a start tag/end tag pair when the element is empty. Instead of writing <Tag></Tag>, the empty element tag <Tag/> can be used. The empty element tag cannot be used if there is any element content, including a single whitespace character.

encoding form   Unicode term that defines how a character is represented in bits. XML supports UTF-8 and UTF-16.

end point   XPointer term indicating the final point that defines a range. See also *start point*.

end tag   The closing delimiter of an element. Each end tag in a well-formed XML document must have a matching start tag.

ending resource   XLink term for the resource that is the destination of a link expressed in an XLink linking element in the starting resource.

evaluation context   XPointer term corresponding to (and extending) the XPath concept of a context. An evaluation context consists of a location (the context location), a nonzero position, a nonzero context size, a set of variable bindings, a library of functions, a namespace binding context, and (where applicable) properties for the values returned by the `here()` and `origin()` functions.

expanded name   Namespace term for a name consisting of the namespace URI and the local part of the QName of the element node or other node.

expression   Term used in XPath to express how to address a selected part of the in-memory representation of an XML document. The most commonly used type of XPath expression is the location path.

external parsed entity   An external entity whose content can be parsed by an XML processor.

external subset   The part of the DTD that is contained in a separate file from the XML document to which it applies. The location of the external subset is indicated within the Document Type Declaration.

fragment identifier   An identifier for a part (fragment) of a document, including XML documents. See *XML Pointer Language*.

general entity   An entity used within the document element. A general entity may be a parsed entity or an unparsed entity.

here() function   XPointer function that returns the context location.

i10n   Abbreviation for *localization*.

i18n   A widely used abbreviation for *internationalization*.

inbound   XLink term that refers to a link where the linking element is expressed on the ending resource.

indicative namespace prefix   The namespace prefix typically used with elements from a particular namespace. For example, the indicative namespace prefix for XSLT is xsl.

information item   A part of the XML information set. An item is broadly equivalent to a node in other models.

information set   An abstract data model that represents the information contained in an XML document as a *set* of information items.

infoset   Abbreviation for the XML Information Set.

instance document   A document that is an example of a class of XML documents, whose structure is defined by a schema that can be a DTD or a schema expressed in XML.

instantiate   XSLT term used to refer to the processing of an XSLT template.

instruction   XSLT term referring to an XSLT element that is contained within an XSLT template.

instruction element   Synonym for an XSLT instruction.

interface   Collection of properties and methods that can be implemented by one or more objects.

internal subset   The part of the DTD that is contained within an XML document. See also *external subset*.

link   XLink term for an association between two or more resources.

linkbase   XLink term, short for link database, that uses extended links of inbound and third-party types.

linking element   XLink term for an element from a non-XLink namespace that has XLink attributes expressing an XLink link.

literal result element   An element not in the XSLT namespace that is contained in an XSLT stylesheet. The literal result element is output literally in the result document (output document).

local part   The final part of a QName that follows the colon character.

local resource   XLink term for a resource that is an XLink linking element or that has an XLink linking element as its parent.

location   XPointer term that includes XPath nodes and XPointer points and ranges.

location path   XPath expression that returns a node set.

location set   XPointer `xpointer()` scheme term referring to an unordered set of XPointer locations. A location set is a generalization of the XPath notion of a node set.

location step   A part of an XPath location path that consists of an axis specifier, a node test, and an optional predicate.

LRE   Abbreviation sometimes used to refer to a literal result element.

markup declaration   In a Document Type Definition, the declaration of elements, attributes, entities, and so on as being present in the permitted structure of a class of XML documents.

named template   An XSLT term that refers to an `xsl:template` element that has a `name` attribute and that can be called by name using `xsl:call-template`.

namespace   In XML, is a collection of names identified by a uniform resource identifier (URI).

namespace declaration   XML 1.0 term indicating an attribute that associates a namespace prefix with a namespace URI.

namespace name   Synonym for the namespace URI.

namespace prefix   The initial part of a QName that is followed by a colon character and the local part.

namespace URI   The unique identifier of an XML namespace. Also called a namespace name. The namespace URI together with the local part form the expanded name of a node.

NCName   An XML name that does not contain a colon character (`:`). Both the namespace prefix and the local part of a qualified name are NCNames.

node   Term used in the Document Object Model and the XML Path Language (XPath) to indicate a logical component of an XML document. Nodes may represent elements, attributes, or other structures present in an XML document. The term node is also used in XPointer.

node-point   An XPointer `xpointer()` scheme point consisting of a point relative to a container node that can have child nodes.

node-set   An unordered set of XPath nodes. The result of applying an XPath location path.

node test   One of three parts of an XPath location step. The first part is the axis specifier, the second is the node test, and finally is an optional predicate. The node test refines the selection of nodes made by the axis specifier.

origin() function   An XPointer function.

outbound   An XLink term used to refer to a link with a local starting resource and a remote ending resource.

output document   A synonym for the result document.

output tree   An XSLT term; a synonym for the result tree.

parameter entity   Entity declared and used within the Document Type Definition.

parent element   Element that contains another XML element nested between its start tag and its end tag (without any intervening level of nesting). The element so nested is termed a child element.

parsed entity   Entity used within the document element of an XML document. A parsed entity is always a general entity.

pattern   An XPath expression that evaluates to a node set. Commonly, a pattern is used to specify which nodes a template is applied to.

point   XPointer `xpointer()` scheme term, indicating a precise point (for example, between two characters) in an XML document. An XPointer point type is broadly equivalent to a DOM Level 2 position.

pointer   XPointer term indicating a string that conforms to the XPointer Framework specification.

pointer part   XPointer term referring to part of a pointer that consists of a scheme name and pointer data that conforms to the specification of that scheme.

position   DOM Level 2 term broadly equivalent to an XPointer point.

post schema validation infoset   The information set of a document that has been validated using the W3C XML Schema specification by a conforming processor. The post schema validation infoset contains additions to the infoset that describe the results of the validation attempt.

predicate   Optional part of an XPath location step that filters the node set selected by the axis specifier and the node test.

principal node type   XPath term that specifies the type of XPath node selected in an axis by default. For example, in the child axis, the element node is the principal node type.

processing instruction   XML processors pass information to associated applications by means of processing instructions that consist of a target (which identifies the application to which the information is to be passed) and a sequence of characters that is the information passed to the application.

PSVI   Abbreviation for the post schema validation infoset.

public identifier   A globally applicable way of identifying the external subset of a DTD. The public identifier is always accompanied by use of a corresponding system identifier.

qualified name   A name consisting of a namespace prefix, followed by a colon character and then a local part.

QName   Abbreviation for *qualified name*.

range   XPointer xpointer() scheme term. A range is measured between two points. A range is similar to what can be selected by dragging across XML text onscreen. A range can span more than one node.

RELAX NG   A schema language expressed in XML syntax. It is an alternative to W3C XML Schemas.

remote resource   XLink term for a resource that participates in an XLink link and that is addressed using a URI reference.

result document   The document produced as the result of applying an XSLT stylesheet to a source document. Also called an output document. The result document is produced by serializing the result tree.

result tree   The in-memory hierarchical structure produced by an XSLT transformation. This structure typically represents an XML, HTML, or other document.

root element   A synonym for the document element.

schema   A document that describes the permitted structure of a class of XML documents. In XML 1.0, the Document Type Definition (DTD) is the specified schema. Alternatively, schemas may be expressed in XML syntax, as in W3C XML Schemas or RELAX NG.

scheme   XPointer term that refers to a pointer data format that has a name and is defined in a (W3C) specification.

shallow copy   In XSLT, copy made when an element is copied without its content.

simple type   One of two types of element content allowed in W3C XML Schemas. If an element has only text content and no attributes or child elements, it is of simple type. See also *complex type*.

source document   XSLT term referring to the XML document to which an XSLT transformation is applied.

start point   XPointer term indicating the point at the beginning of a node or a range. See also *end point*.

start tag   The opening delimiter of any content that an element might have. Each start tag (except for the special case of the shorthand tag for an empty element) must have a matching end tag.

starting resource   XLink term for the resource on which an XLink linking element expresses a link.

style sheet   Term used in Cascading Style Sheets (CSS) to refer to a set of CSS rules. These rules may be embedded within an HTML or XML file, or they may reside in an external file.

stylesheet   Term used in XSLT to refer to an XSLT file. Note that it is one word, compared to the two words used in a CSS style sheet. Sometimes called a transformation sheet.

SVG   Abbreviation for Scalable Vector Graphics. SVG is an application language of XML intended to describe two-dimensional vector graphics.

system identifier A URI reference contained in the Document Type Declaration that indicates the location of the external subset of the DTD.

template XSLT term indicating a collection of instructions nested in an `xsl:template` element.

test XPointer term that corresponds to an XPath node test, generalized to include points and ranges.

third party XLink term that refers to a link where the XLink linking element is in neither the starting resource nor the ending resource.

top-level element A potentially misleading XSLT term that refers to elements that are child elements of the `xsl:stylesheet` element.

transformation sheet A synonym for an XSLT stylesheet.

traversal XLink term for following or using an arc in an XLink link.

Unicode The encoding scheme used by XML. Unicode has both 8-bit and 16-bit encodings used by XML. It also has supplementary code points that allow about one million characters to be encoded. See `www.unicode.org` for further information.

uniform resource identifier See *URI*.

unparsed entity An entity referenced from an attribute declared to be of type `ENTITY` or `ENTITIES`. Such an entity is not intended to be parsed by an XML processor.

URI Abbreviation for uniform resource identifier. A reference to a resource.

UTF-8 Unicode term indicating an encoding form that must be supported by conforming XML processors and that encodes character points in 8-bit numbers.

UTF-16 Unicode term indicating an encoding form that must be supported by conforming XML processors and that encodes character points in 16-bit numbers.

W3C XML Schema Officially called simply XML Schema. W3C XML Schema is the W3C language for expressing XML schemas.

well-formed   XML documents are said to be well-formed when they satisfy the well-formedness criteria, including nesting start and end tags correctly.

whitespace   In XML, a collective term for the space character (#x20), the carriage return character (#x9), the line feed character (#xD) and the tab character (#xA).

XML Pointer Language   A language specified by the W3C that provides a fragment identifier syntax for XML documents.

XML Schema   A slightly ambiguous term that can refer, when written as XML Schema, to the W3C XML Schema specification specifically, or, when written as XML schema (initial lowercase), to a single schema or to XML schema languages generically.

XPath   The XML Path Language. XPath uses a non-XML syntax and is used to address selected parts of a source XML document.

XPointer   Abbreviation for the XML Pointer Language.

XPointer framework   W3C specification that provides a framework for the XPointer schema specifications.

XPointer scheme   One of three syntax options that can be included in XPointer expressions. The three XPointer schemes are `xpointer()`, `xmlns()`, and `element()`.

XSD Schema   Also called W3C XML Schema.

XSLT   Extensible Stylesheet Language Transformation language. XSLT is used to transform an XML document, or selected parts of it, into another XML document or a document in another syntax, such as HTML.

XSLT namespace   The namespace URI for the XSLT namespace is `www.w3.org/1999/XSL/Transform`.

XSLT template instruction   Any element in the XSLT namespace that occurs inside an `xsl:template` element.

INDEX

SYMBOLS

' (apostrophe), 25, 57
* (asterisk) wildcard, XPath axes, 108
@ (at sign), XPath (XML Path Language), 108, 111
+ cardinality operator, 181
: (colon), 31-32, 93-96
, (comma), declarations, 163
{ } (curly brackets), 162-163
:: (double colons), XPath (XML Path Language) axes, 107
// (double forward slashes), 125
" " (double quotation marks), 25, 38
= (equal sign), 25, 96
! (exclamation mark), 67-68
/ (forward slash), 86, 104, 107
([opening parenthesis], pointer parts, 181
. (period), 32, 162
; (semicolon), 57, 71, 163
" (single double quotation mark), quot entity reference, 57
_ (underscore), names, 31
- (hyphen), names, 32
-- (double hyphens), character string, 21
--> ending delimiter, 20, 36
---> ending delimiter, 21, 36

<![CDATA[starting delimiter, 26
< (left angle bracket), lt entity reference, 57
< character, none in attribute values, 35
< > (angle brackets), HTML (Hypertext Markup Language), 9
> (right angle bracket), gt entity reference, 57
<? starting delimiter, 21
<!-- starting delimiter, 20
?> ending delimiter, 21
] (right square bracket), closing delimiter (DTD internal subsets), 45
[(left square bracket), opening delimiter (DTD internal subsets), 45
]]> ending delimiter, 26
& (ampersand), amp entity reference or parsed entities, 57
&# (decimal notation), character references, 71
&#x (hexadecimal notation), character references, 71

NUMBERS

1-byte ASCII code, 70
2-byte ASCII code, 70
16-bit ASCII code, 70-72

N

T